Praise for *FINDING DAD*

My good friend, Kara Sundlun, has never been afraid to confront a challenging story, even when it is her own. Just think of what her father would have missed if she hadn't been brave and tenacious enough to pursue, not just her own identity, but his as well.
~ **Mika Brzezinski**, *Morning Joe* on MSBNC, and best-selling author

Kara Sundlun fearlessly shares her story in efforts to help others. Kara's truth is poured onto each page. We can all take home great messages from this book.
~ **Gabrielle Bernstein**, *New York Times* bestselling author of *Miracles Now*

Kara's story reflects a remarkable personal journey of self-discovery and the powerful connection she had with a father she had yet to meet. Kara's journey takes us through an emotional first meeting with her prominent father to her triumph in nurturing this new relationship for herself and her children.
~ **Donna Palomba**, co-author *Jane Doe No More*, founder of Jane Doe No More, Inc.

Kara's journey to find her father is a compelling story of forgiveness. Anyone struggling with an unresolved relationship will see how healing can begin by taking the single brave step of giving someone a chance at redemption.
~ **Denise D'Ascenzo**, Emmy Award winning news anchor WFSB-TV

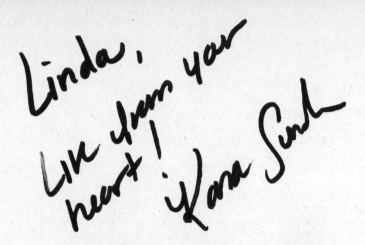

Linda,
Live from your heart!
Kara Sund...

FINDING DAD

FROM "LOVE CHILD" TO DAUGHTER

by
KARA SUNDLUN

Behler
PUBLICATIONS
USA

Behler Publications

Finding Dad: From "Love Child" to Daughter
A Behler Publications Book

Library of Congress Cataloging-in-Publication Data

Sundlun, Kara, 1975-
  Finding Dad : from "love child" to daughter / by Kara Sundlun.
    pages cm
  ISBN 978-1-933016-45-0 (paperback) -- ISBN 1-933016-45-0 (paperback) 1. Sundlun, Kara,
1975- 2. Sundlun, Kara, 1975---Childhood and youth. 3. Sundlun, Bruce G., 1920-2011--
Family. 4. Fathers and daughters--United States--Biography. 5. Illegitimate children--United
States--Biography. 6. Women television journalists--United States--Biography. 7. Governors--
Rhode Island--Biography. 8. Paternity--United States. I. Title.
  CT275.S9665A3 2014
  306.874'2092--dc23
  [B]
                          2014023987

FIRST PRINTING

ISBN 13: 978-1-933016-45-0
e-book ISBN 978-1-933016-24-5

Published by Behler Publications, LLC
USA
www.behlerpublications.com

Manufactured in the United States of America

To Mom, for her unwavering love always.
To my husband, Dennis, and children, Helena and Julian
for being my dream come true.
To my father, for making it all better.

Table of Contents

We are becoming a Fatherless America. It is the epidemic few are talking about, but one that is drastically affecting our homes, health, and yes, our economy. The latest census figures show 43% of American children are living in homes without their fathers. One third of births are now occurring outside of marriage, with many fathers having no connection to their children. President Barack Obama, himself fatherless, started a White House Task Force on Fatherlessness saying, "It is something that leaves a hole in a child's life that no government can fill."

Finding Dad is a call to action. In her riveting memoir, my friend and fellow journalist, Kara Sundlun, addresses one of the most important issues of our time. Kara tells her deeply personal story of the pain caused by not having a father in her life as she grew up in the Midwest with a devoted single mother who, like so many others today, tried to fill the void left by a father who refused to acknowledge his daughter — until Kara forced him to.

Kara's story is a happy ending. She experienced something powerful — her father's acceptance — and that helped her become the empowered woman she is today. Kara will tell you she doesn't believe she could be the successful wife, mother, Emmy award winning television news anchor, and talk show host she is today if she had not been able to connect with her father, whom she calls the "other half of me."

Kara offers valuable lessons as fathers continue to disappear from the American family landscape. Though Kara's story became more public than most, it is one that is all too familiar to communities rich and poor across the nation. *FINDING DAD* shows us fathers can no longer be accessories in the lives of our children if we want a healthy, empowered, and prosperous America.

Kara talks about how the absence of a father left her with a cracked foundation, making her feel less than. In my book, *KNOWING YOUR VALUE*, I urge women to take a stand for what they want, and get what they deserve. But *KNOWING*

YOUR VALUE is a difficult task for a generation of kids who have grown up with one parent refusing to value them at all. Fatherless children are at a dramatically greater risk of drug and alcohol abuse, mental illness, suicide, poor educational performance, teen pregnancy, and criminal behavior, with 85% of youths in prison growing up in a fatherless home, according to the U.S. Department of Health and Human Services.

Kara shows how the entry of a father into her life helped her transform, and she reveals a powerful lesson that it is never too late to heal fractured relationships when we choose to live in the present moment. *FINDING DAD* speaks to the importance of fathers raising their families, and sends the universal message that it's never too late to forgive. It can often take a lifetime to find out who you are and what you are made of. Kara started early. She knew her value. Her journey is a fascinating and powerful look at a young woman's quest to find answers — and herself.

~ **Mika Brzezinski**, *Morning Joe* on MSBNC, and best-selling author

"I cannot think of any need in childhood as strong
as the need for a father's protection."
~ Sigmund Freud

1 The Awakening

Election Night, 1988

I was thirteen years old and had never even seen a picture of my father, when suddenly the invisible character of my childhood had a face. I don't know what woke me up that night, but my eyes popped open with a sense of urgency at the very second a CNN news anchor was announcing the results of the 1988 gubernatorial election in Rhode Island.

"It was a close one in the Ocean State for Bruce Sundlun," she announced. She talked about how this war hero/business tycoon-turned politician had captured forty-nine percent of the vote...almost beating the incumbent, Governor Edward DiPrete.

Seeing his picture staring back at me on TV, Bruce Sundlun was suddenly real, and not just a faceless man who broke my mother's heart. I reached over and shook my mother, who was sleeping next to me. "Mom, wake up! Is that him?" I shrieked.

Bleary eyed from the move to a new house which had us spending the night in a hotel, she looked up and answered me in a scratchy, shocked voice, "He must have gone back to Rhode Island, where he's from."

She hadn't laid eyes on Bruce Sundlun, the man she always referred to as my biological father, since 1977 when she was forced to settle her paternity suit out of court after he refused to claim me as his flesh and blood. There was no such thing as a DNA test back then, the blood tests could only show my father and I both had the same "O" blood type. His big-time lawyers argued the evidence was "inconclusive." Mom eventually caved, and agreed to a $35,000 dollar settlement, and promised to never contact him again, or let me use his surname.

My creators met in the glamorous world of aviation in the 70s when flying was still about the coolest thing you could do on earth. My father was the hot shot CEO of Executive Jet Aviation, a private jet company for the rich and famous in Mom's hometown of Columbus, Ohio. Today the company is known as Net Jets, owned by Warren Buffett.

Back then, Mom was a young and beautiful stewardess with long thin legs, memorable red hair, and mysterious near-turquoise eyes. He was tall and handsome with dark curly hair and intense brown eyes to match his strong personality, a trait mom said I inherited. As her new boss, her knees shook when he walked on the Learjet she was assigned to and felt like she couldn't breathe. She "just knew" right then there was something between them.

Bruce Sundlun embodied power. As a young Jewish bomber pilot in World War II, he was the only one in his crew to escape the Nazis when his plane was shot down—the rest were either killed or captured. After the war, he got his undergraduate degree at Williams College before going on to Harvard Law School before becoming a successful federal prosecutor under President Kennedy, and was known for never losing a corruption case. President Kennedy was impressed with his record and later appointed him to lead America's mission to create an international satellite communications system.

President Kennedy was equally impressed with my father on a personal level and had him help plan the inaugural parade. He and Jackie became good friends, and were both accomplished fox hunters in the prestigious Orange County Hunt in Virginia. His résumé looked like God gave him orders to be first in everything, and never take no for an answer.

Since Mom longed for a different life, and flying was her ticket to another dimension, it was hard for her to deny his charisma and intelligence. "I fell madly in love with him, I have never loved anyone more. And if it were not for him, I wouldn't have you."

I had no idea how he really felt about my mother, but I knew we were a problem for him.

Mom had left Executive Jet after leading a strike against my father for higher wages. My father didn't offer enough at the bargaining table, so they all quit. Mom worked on getting her stockbroker and real estate license, hoping to make a better living, and tried to swear off my tycoon father, affirming she didn't need that kind of roller coaster love affair anymore. She moved away to Florida and started dating another man, but my father kept calling. He would send her tickets to fly back to Ohio and visit, even offering to get her an apartment and a Porsche to drive, so long as she promised to be there for him when he was in town. Eventually, Mom came back to Ohio, but got an apartment with her sister.

Then Mom discovered something unbelievable had happened in the several months they were apart. A friend read in the newspaper that my father had gotten married to his third wife, Joy Carter Sundlun, a socialite from Washington DC. Mom was furious and crushed, but my father told her nothing had to change between them. In a moment of weakness she let him back into her life for one night, and here I am.

He met me once when I was a baby. He stared at me while I blurbled "da-da-da," and told Mom I was "going to have personality." Then he got up and left. She called his son, Peter, who was studying nearby at Denison University, and asked him to come meet his new sister. He didn't come over because our father told him to "stay out of it." It became very clear that my father wouldn't do the right thing unless Mom made him, so she filed a paternity suit. It wasn't easy in 1975 for a woman to raise babies alone by choice.

Now, thirteen years later, I was here in a hotel room, surrounded by crumpled white sheets and the blue glow of the TV, suddenly awakened in another way, whether I wanted it or not.

I could not deny this man anymore. He was real; the news anchor proved him to me with a picture and a story. The anchor had moved on to other stories, but I desperately wanted to press "rewind," see it again, and freeze the graphic of his picture.

Was Mom right?

Did I look like him?

All of a sudden he wasn't just a myth. It's not that I doubted Mom, but until this moment it had always been more of her story — her fantasy, her pain, her rejection — something I had refused to learn more about. Maybe it was self-protection. If I refused to listen to the stories of how my father didn't want me, then I could believe he only rejected Mom, and not me. I could fantasize that it was *my* choice to not have him in my life. I didn't need a father since I was the smart, strong daughter of a single mom. Besides, you can't miss what you don't know, right? Except now that some universal force had awakened me in the middle of the night and shown me who my real father was, I couldn't help but wonder if my own life would be changed forever. Would I get that happy ending I loved to watch in after school movies?

Since I now knew *he* was real, I could theoretically go about finding him. What if he had just been waiting for me to call all this time?

I had barely become a teenager and suddenly everything I had ever believed about not needing a dad was flipped on its head. My inner operating system was being rewired with a new impulse to know more about my other half, and a deep desire to create a happy ending that looked more like the life I saw my friends living. Of course, I had Mom's love, but I craved stability and protection, and wondered if a dad could give it to me.

Growing up, Mom had always told me, "You look and act just like *him*."

I'd hated that and would quickly snap back, "No, I look like *you*."

Now I wondered if Mom was right. The newsflash happened so quickly that the picture flashing on the screen moments before was starting to go fuzzy in my mind. I tried to go back to sleep, wondering if just the two of us *was* really enough. I couldn't help but feel incomplete. Noticing something was missing was the first step on my road to healing.

2 Picket Fence Imposters

Seeing my biological father on TV touched the vulnerable place deep down inside that I tried to live above. My bubbly smile hid the shaky part of my center that ached for stability. I couldn't help but wonder if my big powerful father, who'd just shown up on TV, could rescue me and make me feel safe.

For as long as I could remember, the feeling of loss was ever-present, and got worse when I worried. I had learned to build up my armor, but that fearful place never let me fully exhale because I was always waiting for the other shoe to drop. From the moment I landed on earth, my life was rocky.

It wasn't Mom's fault; she tried, but it was just so hard. She worked full time to keep us in our home, stayed up at night with me, all while trying to fight my father in court. He refused to acknowledge the possibility I was his, even though Mom swore I was, and tests showed we had the same blood type. A judge had to issue a bench warrant just to get him to show up in court. The stress was too much and Mom ended up in the hospital for exhaustion. For two months, she stayed at the hospital every night, though they let her come home during the day to see me. When the doctors released her, she had to give up her job as a star salesperson at IBM, and we moved in with Grandma and Grandpa so they could help take care of me.

Grandma and Mom didn't always get along, but I got along with her beautifully. The extra attention felt luxurious. While Mom rested, Grandma cooked my favorite meal of

Mac 'n' Cheese. Grandpa was wonderful and loved feeding me all the grapes my stomach could possibly hold. "More gips, Pow Pow," I squealed from my high chair while holding out my tiny hands.

Our special relationship was cut short when Grandpa, only a young fifty-nine, died suddenly from a bizarre infection. I was only two years old, and sadly can't remember his legendary hugs. Mom was devastated. Even though I was only a toddler, he had been the only man in my life, and I think his sudden passing was another shockwave that created small cracks in my foundation.

A few months later, Mom gave up her fight with my father and settled for $35,000, which she used to buy a little house so we could start a new life together, just the two of us. I loved having her all to myself, but it was different for her—she wanted and needed more.

When I was three, Mom married John Hewes so she could have a partner and I could have a father. He already had two grown children, but promised Mom he would adopt me and treat me as his own—which meant taking his last name. I know Mom was trying to do the right thing for us, but I didn't like it and refused to get happy about their wedding. This was a huge change for me, and it all happened too fast for my young mind to process. Now I had to share her, and I wasn't ready for that.

On the day of their wedding, Mom dressed me up to be the flower girl, but I refused to walk down the aisle. I stood there clutching Mom's gown and begging her to walk with me. I was terrified of losing her. Seeing no other choice, she pried my tiny fingers off of her, and I made the walk down the aisle of the church, trying not to cry. During our Father-Daughter dance, I accidentally peed on John, splattering my white ankle socks and Mary Jane shoes. It was my three-year-old way of saying "I don't like this, or you!"

Everyone was so busy celebrating, I had to go by myself to the bathroom to clean myself up, and I couldn't help but feel forgotten.

It was a feeling I would become more familiar with as Mom tried to balance her life as a mom and new wife. They left on their honeymoon to Mexico, and I wondered if I would still be the most important thing in her life.

After the wedding, Mom was determined to create the picket fence life in our nice colonial home in Upper Arlington, a bucolic suburb of Columbus. She didn't have to work, so she stayed home, honing her interior design skills by decorating our house in seafoam green and peach, which was all the rage in the 70s. I didn't want to call John "Dad," but Mom said I had to since he had adopted me. To this day, I can't get his name off my birth certificate because of some whack adoption laws that make everything permanent, when it shouldn't be.

A couple years later we moved to a nice four bedroom home in Troy, Michigan. Mom decided that staying at home just wasn't for her, so she went back to work. I secretly wished she could be happy making me cookies, like my friends' moms.

In the meantime, John tried to do all the right things like coaching my soccer team and cutting down Christmas trees, but he was an alcoholic, and more often than not he embarrassed me. I didn't want him to be part of my life. Sometimes he would go on a drinking binge and vanish for a few days. I hated the smell of his breath when he came home to say he was sorry and try to read me a bedtime story. He didn't act at all like my friends' fathers, and there were so many times I wished he would stay gone. I was only about seven at the time, but I remember always making sure he got the mismatched silverware and the chipped plate when I set the table. Why couldn't he just disappear?

We may have tried to look like the perfect family with all the right window dressings, but behind the curtains Mom and John fought a lot. One time, it happened in front of my good friend, Jennifer. We were in the third grade and playing in the family room when I heard the screaming start. It got so bad, Mom threw a jar of molasses at him, and the thick dark goo splattered all over the floor. We were playing in the other room when we heard the screams and sounds of shattering glass. It scared Jennifer to tears and she begged to go home. I was sure nothing like that happened in her perfect Mormon home. The searing shame burned inside me and made me want to throw things back at them. I didn't because I didn't want to look any worse than we already did. More than anything, I desperately wanted to look "normal," and this was anything but a *Leave It to Beaver* moment. Mom tried to convince Jennifer they were just acting out a play so she wouldn't want to call her mom. It didn't work, and from then on I always played at her house.

But the worst humiliation was when John hit the school bus while driving drunk. I was nine years old and thought I would die of embarrassment if anyone found out. I couldn't hide and, for some unearthly reason, Mom brought me to court to witness the judge ordering him to stay in jail for the night. I was so ashamed and wished they would keep him locked up. I would rather not have a dad at all than have one whose name ended up in the police blotter.

Mom tried to help him through rehab, and signed herself up for Al-Anon meetings so she could learn not be so co-dependent and heal her "adult-child." She forced me go to Alateen, even though I wasn't even ten years old yet, just to make sure I could "recover," too. Mom always worried about how things I'd witnessed would impact me later in life, and insisted I get preemptive help. I hated having to talk about my feelings to strangers, and just wanted it all to be over.

When they finally got a legal separation, I was thrilled. Life with John had been filled with unpredictable tension and arguments, and more than anything I wanted a *normal* family life. It was a word I thought about a lot as a child.

When I was in the fifth grade, they finally got divorced and after about a year, John Hewes vanished and quit paying the court-ordered child support. Though we had been abandoned for the second time, I told myself we were better off without him. But I knew Mom was terribly upset he wasn't fulfilling his obligation to support us.

It seems my dislike for John wasn't misplaced, since he was also the reason I never saw a photograph of my real father. Mom had saved pictures and newspaper clippings from his various accomplishments to give me once I got older and asked about my biological father. John got drunk one night and burned everything in the box, saying I didn't need to know any of that, since he had adopted me and was my only father now. Mom said John was jealous that my real father was so successful and thought he was a "dirty Jew."

With John gone, my mom was wearing even more hats, and it seemed she was coming unglued. She was constantly busy trying to grow her interior design business, heal her wounds with therapy, and raise me alone. It was too much for her to handle by herself. I thought having John gone meant I'd have more time with her, but she was busy trying to support us, so I saw a lot less of her. I was too young to understand the stress she was going through. All I knew was that I missed cuddling up for movie nights and having her there after I came home from school.

My ten-year-old self started to crack under the stress. I was lonely and always angry. Between my issues and Mom's pressure of supporting us, raising me alone, and going through a divorce, we began fighting a lot. I'd be furious if she was late to pick me up and criticize her for not doing things like all the stay-at-home moms. I was unfair to her, yet I blamed her for anything that was wrong in my life. I know now the chronic ache of abandonment I felt was partly the fault of a biological father who wouldn't claim me as his own—but back then, I looked to Mom to make it all work.

Adding to my stress was that I was being bullied at school. She was the blonde, popular fifth grader who could make or break my day. If she liked me, I was golden. If she decided I was ugly or dumb, or simply not good enough to play with her, she and the other girls would hit me with jump ropes. I would do anything to make her like me, and even invited her on a getaway with Mom. Looking back, I can barely believe that I took my bully on vacation with me!—but between not having a father, the divorce, a distracted mother, and the bullying, my self worth was disappearing. My already weak foundation crumbed, and coping meant doing anything to make someone approve of me because I wasn't strong enough to stand up to everything that was happening in my young world. My rage was always right under my skin, until it finally boiled over like a tea pot on a roaring flame.

One day, after a typical fight with Mom, I finally blew. I ran upstairs to the bathroom and took my mother's pills she used to manage depression. I found the amber colored prescription bottle in her medicine cabinet and took it to my bathroom. The bottle looked about half full, and I wasn't sure how many it would take to have an effect, so I decided to pop thirteen. I didn't really want to die, but I was dying for attention. I swallowed them one by one, quickly gulping water from the sink to wash them down. When I was done, I angrily stomped downstairs and announced, "I took your pills."

"You did what?" she screamed.

"Yep, thirteen of them. Now you won't have to worry about being there for me."

It was an incredibly cruel thing to say, especially to a woman whose heart had already been broken so many times.

The truth was I was hurting and I wanted her to magically fix my broken world. I needed her to really *see* me, to feel like I mattered, to have my hurts validated, rather than just be pushed to the side because life moved at lightning speed.

It was a desperate cry for help, and it worked. Mom's face went pasty white as she ditched her work files and frantically called Poison Control, where the operator told her to get me syrup of Ipecac. She threw me in the car and sped to the pharmacy down the street. When we got home, I remember feeling happy to have her doting hands on me as she forced me to swallow the thick, bitter syrup. We sat together on the cold bathroom floor as I started throwing up, but I couldn't stay awake. The pills had flooded my tiny blood stream, and I was going in and out of unconsciousness.

I have no memory of Mom racing me to the hospital, or the doctors pumping my stomach. They told her that Poison Control had given her the wrong advice, and that she should have rushed me to the ER. The time at home with the Ipecac could very likely have cost me my life. But despite the doctors' fears, I managed to pull through and made a full recovery after a week in intensive care. They let me go home as long as I enrolled in counseling.

As a mother today, I can't even imagine how paralyzing the fear must have been for my mom to know her child tried to kill herself—and almost succeeded—due to bad advice. Moreover, I can't believe I did that to her.

I did the obligatory ten sessions, but didn't want to go after that because it didn't feel normal. I wasn't in therapy long enough to trace back my father's rejection as the reason for this deep void dwelling inside of me. I never told anyone that I had a biological father I'd never met because I was ashamed. Everyone has a father, right? So why didn't I? Why *couldn't* I?

After everything that had happened, I couldn't face returning to school—to the kids, the teachers, my bully—since everyone knew what I'd done. We needed a fresh start.

Mom put the house on the market and we moved to Florida, where she took a temporary design project so we could begin again. Mom decided the best place to go was back to Columbus where most of Mom's family still lived. This would allow her time to rebuild her business and provide a stable home. The best part was that I could grow up near my cousins.

My Aunt Kathy and Uncle Gary were as American as apple pie, and took me in so I could get settled in school while Mom wrapped up her affairs. I was so excited to live with my cousins, Danielle and Brian, who were near my age and the closest thing I had to siblings. Between Aunt Kathy's legendary home cooked meals and Uncle Gary's boat rides on the weekend and love of Ohio State football, I thrived in the warmth of their home, and didn't mind that it was taking Mom a longer than expected to come get me and find a house. While we waited for Mom to come, Aunt

Kathy enrolled me in school for the last few months of fifth grade and took me shopping for school clothes. But Mom never came.

She'd met a new man and was going to be engaged. She was so sorry about the change in plans, but it all happened so fast. Aunt Kathy had opened her heart and home to make a place for me, and truth was that I loved it. Now, I felt like the carpet had been pulled out from underneath my feet.

Mom had no clue. She thought we should be happy for her, but I could tell Aunt Kathy was furious, and so was I. So much for stability. Mom finally came to Ohio and moved me back home to Bloomfield Hills, Michigan, to a rental house near her fiancé. This was supposed to be a temporary arrangement, since he was very wealthy and wanted us to move in with him and his children. In the meantime, Mom said I might as well start sixth grade at my new forever school.

With all the turmoil and moves, I was getting good at adapting, and it was easier to make new friends. For a couple years, life was good. Mom was thrilled that I tested at the 12th grade level, which put me in all accelerated classes, thus bolstering Mom's vision that I was "destined for greatness." But things started to go south with Mom's fiancé, and shortly after I started the eighth grade, we had to move. Again. The only apartment she could find was outside my current school district.

For a while, I just kept going to my regular school, but the administrators found out we had moved and made me leave. After spending the evening crying and fruitlessly begging my mom to let me stay, I started my fourth school in three years. And what was worse, I was starting a month after school had already started, so when I showed up for my first day, the kids were lined up in the hall, waiting to see the "new girl." I felt overexposed, so I slapped on a big smile as I walked toward the front office.

It was the kind of school where most everyone had been friends since preschool, but two bubbly girls, Dayna and Brooke, saved my pre-teen existence by reaching out to me and welcoming me with open arms into their group. As distraught as I'd been about the move, this was meant to be. To this day, Brooke and Dayna are like sisters to me. I couldn't have known then how they'd be there for me during the media firestorm that would brew a few short years later with my father. But it's safe to say that God gave me bookends to hold me up.

Through their warmth and friendship, my fear about not being liked subsided, and I was grateful and excited to be invited to so many things with my new friends. I also loved the stability of Brooke's and Dayna's homes. They had happy homes with loving, caring parents. Though Mom tried to give me unwavering love and encouragement, my soul was missing the other half of the recipe. I wasn't naïve, and could easily see the difference in my friends' homes. I loved the feeling of their family dinners, and envied the simple things like the greetings they got from their dads after coming home from work—the car pulling in, and the squeal of the children running to see Daddy, climbing on him to clamor for their hugs, stepping on each other's words to tell him about their day. I sometimes looked away, feeling embarrassed—I didn't want them to see me standing there and pity me that I didn't have a dad to hug like them.

I know now there is no substitute for the grounding energy of a father, and without it I was like a dinghy tossing about in the ocean, carried away by each passing current, unsure where life would take me, and yearning for the direction that comes from a *Dad Compass*.

To hide my insecurity, I wanted to appear confident and happy, and learned to just smile so no one would feel awkward. Anytime I felt insecure, my smile rescued me, thereby masking my feelings.

After seeing my real father on TV, I knew he was someone I could be really proud of, and I couldn't help but wonder if he could be my hero. Maybe he was wondering where I was, too?

The hole in my heart was what drove me to find him. Not only did I feel like something had always been missing, but my real father was everything I would want to dream up. He was handsome, successful, wealthy, and powerful, and running for Governor, no less.

I thought if I could just meet him, he could say he was sorry and make up for lost time by giving me the rock solid foundation and unwavering stability that I craved. I could lean on him when Mom was troubled, or when bill collectors started calling. He could rescue us, help my mom, and make me feel safe.

3 The Universe Strikes Again

Election Night, 1990

Two years went by without acting on my growing gut feeling that I needed to know my father, but it was getting harder to ignore the whispers of my soul as they grew louder. I couldn't shake the feeling that I had to meet him. In a practical sense, I didn't know how to find him, since this was pre-Google. I had no idea what had happened to him after he lost the election. Plus, this had been such a huge secret for so long, that I didn't know how to share it with my friends.

The simple explanation to Brooke and Dayna was that my mother was divorced, and I didn't see my father. I left out the part that I technically had two dads from whom I was estranged, and that I'd never met my biological father. The very term "biological father" seemed like an ailment, a wart that that would make me even more different from my friends. While I waffled, the Universe struck again. On TV.

This time it sent me a clear message just as I happened to be walking by the television on Election Day, November 6, 1990. I was fifteen years old.

"On his third try, Rhode Island businessman and war hero, Bruce Sundlun, beat incumbent Governor Edward DiPrete by a landslide," said the CNN news anchor.

Like the big eye in the room, the television was, once again, working as a divine messenger. It seemed someone really wanted me to make a connection. All I'd done is set the intention, and the Universe provided. Via CNN, no less.

Wow, did my dad just become the Governor?

Despite what I do today, I was anything but a news junkie as a teenager and generally watched after-school specials, so I wondered if this CNN intervention was a sign, like God knocking on my head again, urging me to look at the TV, and saying "This time do something, would ya!"

I had no excuses. Even though there was no internet back then, it wouldn't be hard to just call information to get the State House address and phone number.

The idea of contacting my father made me think about how Mom had always said I was "destined for greatness," in part because of his genes. Was I really was just like him, like Mom always said?

It reminded me of the time she took me to see *Top Gun* and nudged me every time Tom Cruise did something amazing. "That's what your dad did. He was a famous fighter pilot."

Apparently, my love of horses was because of him as well. "You know, your father was a champion foxhunter with Jackie Kennedy," Mom would say.

I loved to dive off the high dive, and ride roller coasters, and Mom always told me my fearlessness came from my father, since she was terrified of heights. Ever since her crash in a Learjet while working for my father, she could barely go on the Ferris wheel. A flock of seagulls got sucked into the engine, causing the plane to take a nosedive deep into Lake Erie. Mom almost quit her job as a stewardess right then, but something made her keep working for my father. She loves to tell the story about how she swam to shore without getting her hair wet, and still used her wet green stamps at the store. Add the fact that both my parents survived plane crashes as another thing on the list of my life that makes me a bit different, and all the more "meant to be," as Mom would say.

After my second brush with my father on TV, I couldn't help but think that meeting him was meant to be. My old self defensive belief that I didn't need a father was losing traction, and I could no longer ignore my overwhelming desire to meet him. I constantly envied the father-daughter relationships and stability my friends had. I was good at hiding it, but not having a father made me feel defective and less than whole. I wasn't aware of it then, but the fear of abandonment was so ingrained in me, that I always strived for approval. Like a two-legged stool, I wobbled on the inside trying to compensate for what was missing by trying to be perfect, making the honor roll, excelling in sports, always trying to do better, since just being *me* never felt good enough.

In my Annie-like fantasy, I told the girls my dad was a governor, and I was flying going off to meet him, since he was dying to make it all up to me now that he knew where I was. I imagined what it would be like to have a powerful father who could protect me and teach me about the world. I loved how Brooke's father, who owned a big company, would cheer her on at our soccer games, and take her on great vacations to see the world. Hers was a storybook life; he was powerful and important, and her mom smiled all the time and made the house beautiful with hydrangeas, and home-cooked lemon mint pasta dinners that looked like they were right out of a magazine. It made me wish my mom didn't have to work so hard.

Dayna's dad was always worried about us and had an over-protective nature that Dayna sometimes felt stifling, but I vicariously loved the protection. I yearned for a life right out of a Rockwell painting, complete with a father who would worry about what boys were trying to take me out, and stay up making sure we came home by curfew.

I wondered if my real father could give me what I was missing. Since I now knew exactly where to find him, I had the chance to start erasing the past and create a new future that mirrored the realities I envied—like the orphan who imagines her parents are better than they are, I glossed over his rejection, and fantasized my father would be perfect if I just gave him the chance to do things right. I could have a dad that I would be proud of, and life could be even better than normal, since he was famous and powerful. I could go to the college of my dreams, maybe an Ivy League, like my father. Shouldn't he want to right his mistakes? The fairytale in my mind was growing wings.

Mom gave me her support saying, "I don't want anything to do with him, but he's your father. If you want to reach out to him, I will help you."

I was almost seventeen when I reached a point where my desire to meet my father trumped any fear of rejection, and I decided to just go for it.

In May, 1992, four years after seeing him for the first time on TV, I sat down at our dining room table with Dayna and wrote the letter I had been thinking about for years. She and I did everything together, and I wanted her help with what to say.

Just reaching out to my father didn't seem good enough, and I felt the need to prove myself to this larger-than-life man, even though he had never proved to me he was worthy. Regardless of the outcome, I needed to make a move and get over my fear of rejection and abandonment. I felt shackled by feeling I needed to strive for everyone's approval and acceptance, which ended up with me taking more crap than I should have — be it a bully, or a father who didn't want me. I was so enamored of my fantasy that I skipped over any feelings of hurt. Instead, I wrote in my best cursive on resume stock paper, even placing lined notebook paper underneath to keep my handwriting straight.

This is a bit of what I wrote:

Dear Bruce,

This letter is to inform you that you have a daughter who happens to be intelligent, beautiful, ambitious, and in serious trouble.

Nothing gets attention like teenage drama. The "serious trouble" referred to needing help for college.

Lately, I have had a strong interest in meeting you. If not for anything else, then to see what the other half of me is like. Bruce, I am one of your children, I hope you choose not to ignore this, because I think you would be proud of how I turned out. If you choose to disregard this letter, I assure you

it will not end here. It took a lot of courage to write to you
after seventeen years, and I won't give up on the first try.
Sincerely,
Kara K. Hewes

I included an extra page with some facts about me, as if I really
was writing a resume:
5'2"
Blonde, Green Eyes (like my mom's)
3.75 in West Bloomfield High School
National Honor Society
Very outgoing....

I went on to list anything I thought might make him like me
and respond. Just being his daughter didn't feel like enough. I
know now that feeling "less than" is a text book symptom of
fatherlessness, but back then I just wanted to win over my hero
so he could see I was worthy of acceptance.

Dayna and Mom read it and approved, so I stuck the stamp
on it, marked it personal, and mailed it to Governor Bruce
Sundlun at the Rhode Island State House.

I figured I had nothing to lose, and hoped he would write
back soon.

I never got a response. I would later discover my letter was
stamped "Received May 6, 1992." I spent months wondering if
the letter had gotten lost amidst the influx of citizen complaints
and gala invitations to the Governor's office. I couldn't imagine
he would just ignore such an important letter, and part of me
wanted to assume he just didn't get it. Mom admitted that she
had written him about his medical history after I was
hospitalized for a rare blood disorder when I was four. Even
though I was paralyzed from the waist down for three days with
mysterious bruises all over my legs, he never answered her
letter. Fortunately, the condition cleared up after a few days at
the Children's hospital.

In spite of my not hearing back from him, my life as a high
school junior just went on with homecoming dances, football

games, debate competitions, tests, and quizzes. But the quest to meet my father was set in motion and, as I had told him in my letter, I knew nothing would stop me from making that happen.

4 Time to Get a Lawyer

After months of hearing nothing, the reality of my father's rejection was coloring my fantasy, but I still had an unshakable feeling that if I could just meet him, he would have a change of heart. Mom knew if I really wanted to get my father's attention, we would need an attorney. Since my father had already rejected me as a baby through his high-powered lawyers, it would take someone strong to tackle a sitting Governor. She chose Arthur Read, a well-known leader in the Rhode Island Republican Party who, she believed, would not be intimidated by a sitting democratic Governor. Before taking our case, Mr. Read wanted to meet me, to determine if I was the real deal, or simply someone looking to cash in.

He flew me out to Rhode Island, where I spent the night in his lovely home in the quaint New England town of Barrington. It was my first time to the East Coast, and it felt strange to be sleeping in the same state as my father. The moist air made my hair curl and my skin dewy, and I knew why they called it the Ocean State. His wife's smile was warm as she brought us some snacks and drinks, while Mr. Read talked to me in their living room, trying to size me up.

I explained I wanted to get to know my father and hopefully have a "real father-daughter relationship." At the very least, I also thought he should help with my college expenses. I believed the deal Mom signed at my birth was unfair. Being forced to accept a small lump sum for my life was a pittance compared to the realities of raising a child. Mr. Read agreed, in both a legal and a moral sense. After determining I was the real deal, he agreed to take my case, and a more forceful letter writing campaign began. I couldn't help but feel excited knowing that someone besides Mom thought I was right and validated my desire to meet my father.

Mr. Read called it my, "Arthurian quest."

I didn't want to admit I had no idea what that meant, so I was relieved when he explained the hero legend about Arthur, who didn't know his father was a king and had fathered him out of wedlock. Legend says Arthur was the only one in the land who could draw a sword out of stone, and he fulfilled the prophecy, and took his rightful place on the thrown.

I, too, wanted to pull the sword out of the stone and take my place in my father's life. But I worried that if I caused any epic problems, he would shut me out before I had a chance to touch his heart. Mom and I stressed to Mr. Read the need to tread lightly and avoid any sensationalism that would come if the story of my existence surfaced while he was a sitting Governor. That meant no lawsuits for now.

I hoped that Mr. Read's letters imploring my father to get a DNA test and agree to a meeting would do the trick. I believed if my father just knew I was his flesh and blood, he would claim me.

If I proved myself, how could he not do the right thing and take responsibility?

I was wrong. My father's attorney, Robert Flanders, responded coldly to the letter and didn't agree to do anything, which made me mad. Wasn't he the least bit curious about me? Even though I was only seventeen, I knew this whole runaround was an injustice, and I wasn't going to give up that easily. One day, while I was alone at home after school, my teenage impulsiveness took over and I threw caution to the wind. Forget the lawyers; I decided to try to get my father on the phone myself.

Back then, when you needed a number quickly, you called information, so I pounded 1-555-1212, into our 90s style cordless phone and asked for the number for the Governor's office in Rhode Island. I dialed it fast so I wouldn't change my mind. The operator at the State House answered and I pretended to be someone my father knew. I deepened the tone of my voice so I'd sound more like an adult. "This is Kara Hewes, the Governor will know what it's regarding."

Surprisingly, I was put through to the Governor's executive assistant, Patti Goldstein, who answered the phone in a friendly, disarming voice. I never expected to get this far, and my heart nearly leaped out of my chest. It was my turn to speak, and I had no plan of what I would say, so I just punted. I told her I'd sent a letter and would like to meet the Governor, whom I believed was my father.

Patti seemed to know all about me and was aware of the attempts to schedule a meeting with my father. Her voice was soft and sweet, and she talked to me like I was a child, trying to make me understand his schedule was so busy with the upcoming election and all. "Bruce does want to meet you, he just couldn't possibly do it right now."

Something in me made me want to scream "This is bullshit!" Instead, words I didn't expect flowed out of my mouth from a deep, powerful place. I told her I was coming to Rhode Island to look at Brown University as a possible choice for college, and since I was going to be there anyway perhaps he could spare a moment in his "busy schedule."

Patti's sweet, mom-like voice asked if there was any way we could schedule another time, since they were so booked leading up to Election Day.

"No." I wouldn't budge. "I already have the plane tickets for this trip."

I didn't really have tickets, but I felt justified in forcing the issue. I really wanted this, and I wasn't going to back down. I figured if she said yes, I would buy the ticket somehow.

Patti promised to get back to me.

I must have gotten their attention, because soon after, Mr. Read called and told me my father would meet me and get a DNA test. I'd won my first important battle, and I was giddy with excitement. So long as the DNA test came out the way we believed it would, the rest would take care of itself. Or at least I assumed it would.

5 The Secret Meeting

October 25, 1992

This was the day that everything I'd worked for would finally pay off—I would get to meet my father for the first time. My brain was on overload, trying to imagine what it would be like. My adrenaline was pumping as I raced around our apartment trying to get ready. I'm surprised I didn't forget to breathe. My morning started out with my usual routine, a steaming hot shower followed by slathering hair-straightening products into my long kinky-curly blonde hair. My mother was yelling from the kitchen, "Wear your hair curly...like his. He's Jewish, and that curly hair came from him."

I yelled back from my room, "No, I want to wear it straight."

At seventeen, I had mastered the art of using a hot hair dryer and big round brushes to smooth my frizz, and I wasn't about to go curly now. What a strange feeling, making myself look pretty for a man who had provided the DNA that determined how I looked. Would he not like me if I didn't look like him? Even though the frizz was his fault, I didn't want to meet him that way. I wanted to be beautiful, and secretly hoped he would claim me on the spot. I would only get four hours because "the Governor's schedule is so busy." I protected my blow-out with more straightening products and moved on to the next thing on my Meeting Dad To-Do list.

What should I wear to meet my maker?

I wanted to look polished, smart, and East Coast. I wanted to look "good enough" for him—my rich, powerful, Harvard-educated father. I decided to dress like I would for a college interview, hoping I would impress him. The designer clothes I'd scored at the discount stores would come in handy today. My grey wool turtleneck tucked into charcoal grey slacks hit the perfect combination of conservative and feminine, just like I imagined he would want me to be.

Mom tried pulling my head out of the clouds with common sense. "He's going to greet you with his standard, 'Hi, Bruce Sundlun.' He'll shake your hand firmly. That's how he greets everyone."

I told myself if anyone should be nervous, it should be him, and planned to shake it back just as hard.

First, I would have to get there, and as if I wasn't stressed out enough, I realized, as usual, I was running late. Oh God, I couldn't miss my flight! This secret meeting had taken so much time and energy to get. And as late as I was, I was about to meet my father, and I desperately needed my baby book. Crap, where was it? My mother had saved baby pictures, cards, stats from my pediatrician, all information that would sum up the beginning of my life—the days *he* tried so hard not to be a part of. I half thought that he didn't have the right to see this yet, but I considered that it would give us something good to talk about. A conversation piece, like a pretty coffee table book, only this was more of a marketing package to make him like me—make him accept me, and have a real father-daughter relationship.

Here, look at the cute blonde baby you wanted nothing to do with. Look, here's me and my mom at the zoo...after she sued you for paternity and was forced by your big-time lawyers to settle out of court and go away. I know you didn't want me, and made us promise to never call you or use your very important surname, but I just want to show you all the sweet times you missed at Christmas, my birthday, my first day of school. Hey, I hear my brother, Peter, has blonde curly hair, too. Do you want to see my lock of hair in this little envelope? Everyone always tells me I look just like you. Do you think so? Do your baby pictures look like mine? By the way, my hair really is curly, I just make it straight.

After racing around our apartment, I finally found it. The Hallmark-like picture on the cover of a woman cradling a newborn while basking in the glow of love for her new baby had yellowed with age. This cookie cutter memory keeper did not quite fit my life, but it would have to do.

With my baby book and plane tickets in hand, I hopped in my teenage love, my first car, Nissy, a used silver Nissan Sentra, and raced to Detroit Metro airport. I wanted the quiet of driving myself to the airport—free of my mother's reminders to do this or say that. I also needed to avoid questions from any friends who seemed incapable of understanding this experience. This was something I had to do alone, and seven hours from now, I could tell everyone how it went.

My father's people had arranged to fly me into Boston to avoid the possibility of local press in Rhode Island getting wind of our clandestine meeting. Getting off the plane an hour later, I found a young staffer named David holding a sign with my name on it. He was tall and thin with wavy hair, and as we locked eyes, I suddenly looked away as the gravity of what was happening hit me: *Oh God, my father has a staff, and this guy is here to pick me up and keep me hidden.*

David drove me away from Logan airport in a dark blue Crown Victoria that looked like an undercover police car.

I wonder if we're being recorded in this car, like the movies?

We made the hour trip to my father's condominium in Providence for our secret meeting. I learned from David my father didn't actually live there, but used it when he had to work late at the State House and didn't want to drive all the way home to his Newport estate. As he drove, we talked about school, the weather, and basically anything other than why he was driving me to meet the Governor. I wasn't sure what he had been told, and I was scared to make a mistake and say something wrong, so we just chatted about whatever, and I laughed a lot…my way of taking the edge off.

The car came to a stop in front of the historic brick building from the 1800s on South Main Street, and David, unable to stop himself from an unapproved question, asked, "What are you going to talk to him about? He isn't one for small talk."

Truthfully, I had no idea what I would say, I was a talker by nature and hoped the right words would just come out. At least I had my baby book to fall back on.

"I don't know," I confessed, "but I have some pictures."

Patti, the sweet, perky lady who had taken my calls to the State House, answered the door. She had set out popcorn and photo albums of my father's life. *Great, he was ready for Show and Tell, too.* She explained the Governor was a Washington Redskins fan and the team was playing today, so she would put the game on TV in the background. It could have seemed cold, but I felt relieved there would be a distraction, something to focus on if our conversation turned awkward. Our casual snacks didn't match the formal décor. The room was filled with antique end tables and a couch that looked custom made to match the regal drapes. It seemed like a room right out of the White House, and I imagined my father holding high-powered meetings here.

My father entered the room and extended his hand to me. "Hi, Bruce Sundlun." *Wow, Mom got it exactly right.*

"Hi, Kara Hewes, nice to meet you," I said, giving him my best firm handshake. I was too nervous to make real eye contact.

"Nice to see you. Sit down," he said motioning to the fancy couch as if to welcome me.

Breathe, Kara, just breathe.

I tried to look at him without making it seem like I was staring. He was old enough be my grandfather, but looked much younger than seventy-two since he didn't have the wrinkles I expected. Instead, he was tall and handsome, and walked with the intensity of a soldier with his shoulder blades pinched back in his navy blazer as if he was squeezing an apple between them. He was buttoned up in his striped tie, and I could tell he wasn't about to let his guard down. He had a full head of thick, grey-white wavy hair that he slicked back to reveal an intimidating widow's peak. Like a real life Daddy Warbucks, he was powerful, polished, and intense. I couldn't help but feel a little intimidated, but I refused to show it.

The first few moments were awkward. I couldn't remove my reflexive pasted-on smile as he spoke with long pregnant pauses about things I knew nothing about, like the banking crisis in Rhode Island, and how he was fixing it.

"What's that pin for?" I said, trying to break the ice by noticing a green "M" on his lapel.

"This is for my wife, Marjorie. She nearly died a year ago when she was hit by a car in upstate New York."

The pin was for the one-year anniversary of the accident, and celebrated her triumphant recovery. She had fought to walk and talk again, even though doctors said she never would.

"Wow, she must be a strong lady," I said, trying to make conversation.

It was strange to think of him having a wife, since I had only pictured him alone in all of my daydreams.

I knew Marjorie was his fourth wife, and I wondered what happened to the third wife, the one he cheated on with my mom. He talked about how much Rhode Island loved its First Lady for her warm personality, joking that she was much more likeable than he was. I could see the pain behind his eyes. Even though he looked like the tough guy Mom described, my intuition told me there was more to this warrior underneath his rough exterior. Problem was, I wasn't sure how to get to it.

This was new territory for both of us. He didn't know how to talk to a seventeen-year-old girl, and I wasn't sure what to say to a governor. Thankfully, our photo albums were worth way more than a thousand words. He showed me pictures of himself as a young runner and told me he discovered his speed while running away from other kids who wanted to beat him up for being Jewish.

"It taught me that if you have a disability, make use of it," he said with a smile, uttering the piece of advice I would later hear a hundred times more in my life.

He mentioned that he'd have probably gone to the Olympics in 1944 if they hadn't been cancelled for the war. Instead, he dropped bombs over Germany from his B-17 Flying Fortress. I reminded myself again that I was sitting next to a real life hero. Wow.

His fierce energy may have scared others, but it was exactly what I needed in my life to feel safe. Like a guard dog, his bark could instill fear in outsiders with just a look, but I wanted to be an insider, so his growl could protect me.

He spoke to me in a kind, but formal tone, as if he was giving a lecture. I know now that he felt comfortable in the role of leader and teacher. He loved to hold court like a king, and being in charge allowed him to build a protective moat around his heart.

I looked at his photos, trying to see the man behind them. His boyhood pictures looked almost angelic with soft curly hair and innocent eyes, but his face hardened as we turned the pages. His life was marked by battles that he always seemed to win, but I couldn't help but wonder at what cost? Here I was sitting next to him, a casualty of his fight to not be a father because it didn't suit him, and all we did was dance around the big white elephant that I could be his daughter.

Yet, I could feel his approval as I showed him awards from school, and told him I was a straight A student. His eyes widened as he looked at my accolades, "You have an impressive record for such a young lady."

Wow, he likes me, and I like him.

As I pointed to a picture to explain what he was seeing, my hand briefly touched his by accident. I felt a rush of electricity. My God! He was real, and this was actually happening!

Though he wasn't saying much, a part of me was connecting to the softer side of him, the side he tried to never show. I saw glimpses of it when his eyes softened while looking at my pictures. There was an unspoken transfer of energy as we talked about our lives, as though we saw our reflection in each other. He was the other half of me. In fact, later, my new family would joke that I was the female version of him. We really were so much alike, and each held the missing piece to heal the other. He could be my rock solid source of stability and safety, and I could be the one to soften his heart. Like a new puppy, I was eager to give him the kind of unconditional love he needed, but never let in.

His smile revealed a hint of pride looking at my varsity ski team pictures and my winning debate record. These were things he was good at, too, and I wondered if he saw himself in me even though we seemed like opposites. I'm already a bubbly person by nature, but my nervousness that day made me smile and laugh more as I tried to tell him stories about my life back home.

As I giggled, he stared at me and said, "You remind me of your mother, she was effervescent too."

Wow, he just mentioned Mom, maybe we were going to talk about why I was here?

I grabbed some popcorn and sucked down some pink juice getting ready to move past pleasantries, but it was a false alarm.

Instead, he moved on to pictures from his inauguration, and he showed me my three half-brothers, Tracy, Stuart, and Peter, and, who he referred to only as his sons. I stared at Peter since Mom always told me I looked most like him with his blonde hair and light eyes, but I couldn't be sure. My father's eyes were dark brown, and nothing on his face jumped out and said "I have your DNA." He was fifty-five years older than I, and a man, so it was hard for me to see the striking resemblance everyone would later remark on. I kept waiting for something deep inside to go DING! and let me know for sure this man was really my father. But it didn't. Like him, the rational side of my brain was running the show, and I told myself I would just have to do this one step at time.

He was judging me, too. I'm only 5'2" and wasn't even a hundred pounds yet, so when I stood up to go to the bathroom, he seemed shocked as he looked me up and down.

"You are one of the smallest women I've ever seen. Was your mother that short?" he asked, seeming to question how he could have a daughter as tiny as I was. He was still trying to convince himself I couldn't be his.

"No, she's 5'6", but her mother was short, and I'm told yours was, too." No comment.

My stomach tightened. I had just inched toward the real question of why we were both here sharing our life stories on a Sunday afternoon over juice and popcorn with people listening to us in the other room.

Thank goodness for football so he could look away and yell, "Hot damn, that's a good play."

The game and my bathroom break was a good way for us both to take a breath.

In the bathroom, I tried to collect my spinning thoughts. I wanted him to be the one bring *IT* up, but I realized my time was running out. Soon, the staffer would be back to drive me to the airport, and we hadn't discussed my reason for being here. I finally gathered my guts and went back into the room armed with my question.

"So, do I look like anyone on your side of the family?

Pause.

"No," he said with a good poker face.

My heart sank. Really? Is that it? He doesn't think I'm his? But we seemed to get along so well. The only thing certain was this meeting was almost over, and my plane would be leaving soon.

"Look, they have asked me to take a blood test, so I will take a blood test. We'll get the results and go from there. Regardless, it was nice meeting you," he said matter-of-factly.

He had put so much effort into battling against me, but my stubborn spirit wasn't about to let him win. Despite the barriers he put up, my younger, more open, heart felt something he wasn't revealing.

I kept my smile intact in order to hide the disappointment that sucked the air right out of me. My rational side protected my heart, and I told myself that once we got the DNA results, he would say or do more. I knew we weren't alone, and I could tell he was being careful about what he said out loud. It wasn't until years later that I uncovered a file in his basement and discovered he had been advised by his attorneys to keep his answers to me vague and noncommittal. At the time, I'd have given anything for some telepathic powers to hear his private thoughts and feelings.

We were both infinitely changed at our secret meeting, with that first handshake. It was a major fork in the road of our lives, and an unspoken healing energy was set in motion. I was determined that one day I'd unlock his heart, and he would protect mine. But we had a long way to go before we reached that point.

I thanked him and Patti for the popcorn and walked to the door. The biggest moment of my life was over, and I had no idea what it meant. I held on to the feeling that I just knew he liked me.

David, the staffer, was waiting by the car to take me back to the airport. I didn't want to say too much, but would later learn that David didn't need me to say anything. He'd been holed up in an empty office across the street with other senior staffers and already told them I was clearly my father's daughter. "She looks and acts just like him." He says he saw it in my face, but it was my confidence that reminded him of my father. He thought I was quite poised for a teenager.

I had always been good at covering up my emotions with a smile, but underneath my confident exterior I was just hoping the blood tests would prove Mom had been right.

When I arrived home that night, Mom wanted to know all about my trip. "Did you see that you looked just like him?"

"Not really—maybe—I couldn't really tell."

Mom was dying to know every detail, but I was so overwhelmed by my day, I just wanted to go to my room and be alone to process it all.

"What did he say?"

"He was nice, but very formal. He showed me pictures and shook my hand firmly, like you said he would."

"Yep, that's Bruce. What else?"

"He said that we'd talk more after the DNA test comes back."

Mom instantly got defensive. "Oh, Kara, we don't even need that test. We can get it, but I know you're his, and so does he. He better do the right thing, so help me God."

I was so exhausted, all I wanted to do was sleep, and I couldn't bear to think about what the "so help me" next steps would be if he didn't do the right thing.

Mom would later tell me she saw so much of my father in me that day. "You're blessed with those rational, analytical genes."

While Mom was a bundle of nerves, she told me I'd appeared so calm, and ready for the next step. She's always had difficulty disconnecting from her emotions, but she says my ability to pull the plug comes from my father's wiring.

The following day, I called Dayna and Brooke to tell them how it went. "It was fun, and he was cool, but I don't know what will happen. I'll have to wait for the results of my DNA test."

As kids, we were used to taking tests, but this was one I really had to pass. It was the last hurdle that allowed me to continually give him the benefit of the doubt. Technically, he hadn't rejected me yet, since he didn't really know I was his. At least that's what I told myself.

6 I'm His, Now What?

Mom and I walked into the lab at Beaumont Hospital in Troy to get our DNA test. The phlebotomist asked for our IDs, took our fingerprints and Polaroid pictures of our faces. It was such a surreal experience that part of me wondered what facial expression was appropriate for something like this. Do I smile? Keep it serious? I wondered if this would be the same procedure for my father. Would the Governor need to show ID? Could he rig the test if he wanted to? With his money and power, he had made me go away once before. Could he do it again? Would he?

The wounds of rejection back then were only energetic imprints on my tiny heart, deeply buried. But over time, they had grown. Now there was so much more at stake. This time he would be rejecting *me*, not just Mom. If this test wasn't positive, I would always wonder if my life story was a lie, or if my true identity would be forever hidden by a corrupt nurse. I had seen this play out badly on *General Hospital*.

I clenched my clammy hand to make a tight fist, willing my heart to pump out my very best blood to guarantee the proper results. I felt queasy, knowing the shame would swallow me up if Mom was somehow wrong.

Ten days later, our attorney called to say it was "highly likely" I was Bruce Sundlun's daughter. That was the language on the test result document. When my father heard his lawyer use the term, "highly likely," he said he'd never heard of that in a legal sense.

"So what exactly does that mean?" we asked, equally confused.

It meant that the results were 98.6 percent positive, which in the world of science at that time meant it was as good as it got. He was my father, no ifs, ands, or buts about it. Thank God Mom was right. I could breathe again. Somehow, just knowing this wasn't all a lie meant more than knowing if my father would acknowledge me. I had already won something, and the feeling was tangible, like cement being poured into my shaky groundwork. I looked at all the little letters on the test results that represented chromosomes, and wondered if I could determine exactly which parts of me came from which parent. Wow, I guess that curly hair did come from my Jewish half. Double wow, I guess I really am half Jewish. That big, strong hero was my father.

Now what?

Would we celebrate holidays together? Would my half-brothers like me? How would I get to know this man who'd helped create me? I was excited and relieved, yet so unsure about what this confirmation of identity really meant.

But nothing happened. I received no news from my father about his plans, given the positive DNA test results. He'd easily won his second term for Governor and, apparently, I was not high on the list of priorities. By December, about two months after the tests, I got mad. Christmas was coming, so do I buy him a gift? So far, I hadn't gotten so much as a phone call from him about our confirmed bloodline. Frustrated, I called the State House again. Patti took my call when I asked for the Governor. She tried to calm me down and told me to be patient; my father was just trying to figure out what to do.

"What do you mean he's trying to figure out what to do? I'm his daughter. He's seventy-two years old. If he can run a state, this should be easy!"

I tried to be tough, but instead I felt the tears streaming down my face. My inner unrest had erupted, and there was no more stuffing down my feelings to project my self-created calm, mature demeanor. I was a teenager having a tantrum, and he deserved it. Since he never took my calls, I was exploding on the only one who would send him my message.

"It's not fair!" I cried. "He promised he would do something after the test, and now he knows I'm his daughter, so what's taking him so long?"

Patti didn't have any good answers, but promised to talk to him and let him know I wanted to hear from him.

I was furious and sat down to write another letter, but I had the sense to calm down before pouring my heart out on paper.

> *Dear Bruce,*
> *I have been contemplating writing this letter, but procrastinated for lack of words to say. When I received the blood test, I was pleased, yet not surprised. I never had a doubt the outcome would be positive. My doubts lie with you..."*

I wanted him to know this was a problem he had to handle, and not push it off on his handlers.

> *"Ideally, I'd hope you would feel happy and fortunate to have a daughter, however I understand the complications you are faced with. I want desperately to know you and recognize you as my real father, not just someone who shares my chromosomes. I suppose lawyers are necessary, yet they cannot be depended on for cultivating a relationship. That must come with time from within us.*
>
> *I was impressed by your intellect and accomplishments at our meeting, but I also saw a warm man beneath it all. This is the man I wish to know. Enclosed is a Christmas gift, or should I say Hanukkah? Regardless, Happy Holidays! I'll wait to hear from you. I'm excited to visit again soon. By the way, I won first place in a District Debate competition. Am I born lawyer or what?! Just kidding, Bruce, please write back or call...*
> *Love,*
> *Kara*

I never got a response and was left feeling empty and uncertain about what do next. I'd hoped he would at least send me a card for Christmas, but I got nothing.

It wasn't until later that I learned he'd been on his traditional holiday vacation with my brothers and their families at his villa in Jamaica—and he'd never told any of them about me. I imagine he thought about it, but I know now that he just didn't do emotions. Patti would later confess that I'd frightened him way more than any plane with a shot-out engine. He knew how to handle a crisis, so long as it didn't involve his heart. Just like when he ran from the Nazis—who'd shot down his B-17—he was going to stay underground for as long as possible.

Meanwhile, my mother was furious he was hurting us all over again. On February 10, 1993, two months after the DNA test results, my mother saw my dejection and went into protective mode by faxing a letter to Patti to give to my father. Her intent was to make it clear we didn't want to hurt him, but we needed to hear from him soon.

> *Dear Bruce,*
>
> *This letter is written with total sincerity and as a last measure of good faith. I have been very patient and understanding, to say the least. Now we need to hear from you. Our daughter has turned into an incredible young woman. It's sad you've never had the experience of seeing Kara for what she is (only one meeting). I could never have asked for a better child. Raising her to be who she is has been very difficult...I don't believe you could possibly understand what it must have been like...*

She went on to share some of her own story of surviving as a single parent while trying to build a business. And for the first time, she admitted she needed his help.

> *"Giving Kara all the advantages of good schools takes more money than most single parents can provide."*

She told him he should help pay for my education, and start taking an active role in my life. As much as it pained her, she could see just having a mother wasn't enough for me, and she wanted me to be all I could be.

"Kara, with all of her brains, beauty, and spunk, now needs her father. We must hear from you this month. While I am hoping with all good intentions you are ready and willing to now do your part, I am also prepared to do whatever is necessary if you choose to ignore your responsibilities to me and your daughter..."

Once again, nothing came back. I couldn't believe it. How could he just ignore me?

Our attorney, Mr. Read, tried his luck with a letter to my father's attorney.

"The ball has been in the Governor's court for almost two months now, and we have not had any response...the reality of this case is that either Governor Sundlun is going to face up to this problem and try to respond to it in a reasonable approach, or he is not."

The files I uncovered years later showed my father had no intention of claiming me. While I was pouring my heart out, his lawyer was sending him case law, citing reasons why he didn't owe me anything, since my mother had taken his crappy settlement and I'd been adopted by another man.

He did tell our attorney he would help me with college but, to him, that meant dictating a few letters—not agreeing to help with expenses. On February 25, 1993, fifteen days after Mom faxed her letter, my father wrote a letter to the assistant director of admissions at Boston University saying,

"Kara is someone whom I know personally as a very intelligent, vivacious and highly motivated young person."

He managed to leave out the part that I was his daughter when asking that every consideration be given to my application.

A similar letter was sent to the Governor of Michigan, John Engler, urging him to help me get in to the University of Michigan, since I was a "remarkable student."

The timing of all the letters and calling me a "friend" made it clear my father did not plan on acknowledging me, and was trying to see how to make all of this just go away. Eventually, an offer did come from his attorney for $1,000 a year and $10,000 when he died, but no admission he was my father.

Really, *Dad?* I bared my soul to you, proved I was your daughter, waited in silence for months, and you're offering me twenty bucks a week? I felt sick. Had I really gone through all this just to be kicked in the stomach with a cheap offer? He was the one being slimy, but I was the vulnerable one. The shame of this insulting offer made me feel all the more unworthy.

My sense of self-preservation had toughened me, and I decided I'd come too far to give up now. I had nothing left to lose. If he didn't want a relationship with me, then I would still fight to make him publicly acknowledge me and help pay for college. My doubts about my father were growing, and I had to prepare myself to either give up, or fight harder. I chose the latter because, as crazy as this sounds, part of me still had faith my father would come around. I believed my identity was worth fighting for.

7 No More Miss Nice Girl

For so long, I just wanted my father to like me, so I'd walked on eggshells by keeping my story a secret from the press, to show him I was genuine about wanting to be acknowledged by him. In spite of the proof that I was his daughter, his rejection roused enough of my anger that I was eager to make my next move—and I wasn't concerned with looking nice. The Mayor of Detroit, Coleman Young, was being sued for paternity, and the stories about his case were leading every newscast. Mom decided it might be a good idea to call in a big gun and meet with the super-lawyer who was going up against the Mayor of Detroit.

I walked into Henry Baskin's big beautiful office in Beverly Hills, Michigan. He seemed kind, yet exuded the kind of cut-throat confidence required to make him the star he was. After a brief conversation of what we had done so far, he pointed to the thick stack of letters, DNA test results, and endless legal memorandums, and gave it to me straight. "Your dad isn't going to do anything unless we make him."

Henry explained that unless I filed a lawsuit by the time I turned eighteen, I would lose any opportunity to force my father to acknowledge me, or pay for college.

This was a huge turning point for me—my destiny just got a deadline, and I couldn't lose my chance to make my father publicly admit that I was his daughter. As improbable as it seemed, I still dreamed of the happy ending. But I was no fool. Barring his acceptance of me, I knew, at the very least, it was important for him to help provide for my education—even if that meant suing him for it.

"Fine," I said, biting my bottom lip, wishing we had a better choice, "let's do it,"

Henry explained how he'd been adopted himself and understood the emotional importance of what I was trying to do. Since it hit close to home for him, he told me he would do the work pro bono, though he made it clear he would not fight for any back support for my mother. It wasn't that she didn't deserve it, but he felt bringing her in would be a distraction, and insisted that the lawsuit focus only on me.

We filed the paternity suit, and the media firestorm began.

Henry sent out a national press release on June 8, 1993, saying an East Coast Governor was being sued for paternity by a Midwestern teenager, and invited members of the media to a news conference at his office the following day.

My father beat Henry to the punch and followed the old political adage that the best defense is a good offense. He held a news conference announcing that he had a teenage daughter in Michigan.

Instead of saying how sorry he was for not being there for me, he attacked my mom and said she was a "gold-digger" who had been after him every time he ran for election—all stinging lies. Mom had nothing to gain, even though she deserved everything. She only signed the lawsuit because I was a minor.

"I met Kara Hewes once in my house in Providence," he said into the podium full of microphones. "We had a very pleasant meeting. She asked for my assistance in getting into various colleges, and I did assist her. The timing of this lawsuit doesn't surprise me, because Judith's daughter, Kara, turns eighteen in about a month, after which there would be no possibility of support obligation, even if she was not already the adopted daughter of another man."

I was sickened. I wanted to scream at the TV. How could he do this?

I thought he would want to help once he knew I was his. Now I didn't know what to believe as I watched him attack my mother on live TV.

He finished by saying, "We shall defend the suit in court."

How could he say he owed me nothing? Even if that was a legal argument, how could he not want to be my father now that we had proven I really was his daughter? Mom angrily turned off the TV and started sobbing over the gold digger accusations. "I hope he does the right thing for you, Kara, but I'm done, and I mean ALL done. I don't need this in my life. He's trying to destroy me all over again."

The clash of my creators was terrifying. I worried Mom would break down, and it would be my fault. What had I done to us?

Mom was so mad she was already threatening to file a slander suit against my father. She was terrified the bad press would ruin her good name and the interior design business she had worked so hard to build. I panicked at the thought of two ongoing lawsuits. "Mom, please, let's just stay calm for now; it'll get better soon."

"Whose side are you on? I'm your mother, you know, or did you forget that?"

Her venom was building with each news story that referred to her as "an affair from the 70s," and like a wounded snake, she was ready to hiss and pounce. I understood her anger, but being around her was poison for me. I was trying to stay calm, and she was anything but.

This was not part of the happy ending Rockwell fantasy I had played over in my mind so many times. My stomach stayed in a perpetual knot as I vacillated between guilt and hope. I felt responsible for my mom's pain over his lies, and wanted to do something—anything—to set the record straight. I never meant for it to happen like this. I never imagined he would try to attack my mother. Since I'd started it, I felt like it was my job to fix it, defend her, and play peacemaker. My young heart was fighting for the most basic human need—love—and it would do anything to find that path. But these unintended consequences made me question if I had done the right thing.

TV would turn out to be the mediator. Thank God for Henry, who told me it would all be okay, that tomorrow would be my turn to alter the tide and tell my truth.

In the meantime, every hour brought a new news story which showed my father being skewered in the press. His denial of any responsibility was not sitting well with the pundits, or the people. The tabloid show *Hard Copy* showed him cornered by reporters right in front of one of his own billboards promising a crackdown on deadbeat dads.

"Governor, are you a deadbeat dad?" the reporter asked.

"No. Now excuse me, I need to get by," he muffled, looking down.

Sure, he'd brought this on himself, but I couldn't help but feel badly for him. I never wanted to hurt him, and now I was really worried whether he would like me. It was easier to feel for everyone else, since I had to detach from my own feelings. If I had succumbed to the emotional tsunami around me, I would have drowned, so I survived by living above it all, and going to a deeper, stronger place that allowed me to put one foot in front of the other. I didn't know it then, but it was a lesson in surrender. I was too mentally exhausted to do anything but just go with the flow. I followed the energy that was in motion, and my gut guided me to have faith. I had no choice but try and trust it. Looking back now I learned that just when you think your world is broken, a breakthrough can happen. I was about to make my dreams come true, but no one, including me, could have predicted the shocker that was coming.

All I knew for certain was that I would get to tell my side of the story on national TV in twenty-four hours. "Tomorrow, it's my turn."

8 My Big Day

June 9, 1993

This was the day I'd ask my father to acknowledge me — on live TV. I was determined not to let his rejection get in the way. Besides, no matter what he tried to say, I was right. There was no doubt he was my father, so why wouldn't he want to help me?

The lawyers and my parents were fighting from their heads, a place where the ego rules, so it was all about who was right or wrong. My naiveté allowed me to stay in my heart, a place that only looked for love that my soul needed.

As I drove to Henry's office for the news conference, my spirit gave me a pep talk.

I know he has a soft spot in his heart, whether he realizes it or not. I saw it the day I met him. I just need to reach it. I know there is more to him, I can feel it. I can feel this is supposed to happen, somehow, it's meant to be.

What will I say to the press?

Driving alone with my thoughts, I focused on what had happened since my press conference. The story of the Governor of Rhode Island and his "Love Child" was already leading all the local and national newscasts, along with the nation's major papers. My father's admission on TV that it was "highly likely" I was his daughter only made the press more determined to find me. Well, ready or not, here I come…

Pulling into my lawyer's parking lot, I saw that it was crammed with dozens of news trucks, reporters, and photographers running around getting ready for the big story — me. Gulp.

Crap, how can I make it inside without being seen? Henry is going to kill me for being late.

I twisted up my long hair — that I'd spent way too much time blowing straight — into a baseball hat, and hot-footed it to the door, holding my breath and hoping no one would spot me.

As I skipped into the building, the impact of my decisions weighed heavily on me, and I could only hope I was doing the right thing. Then again, it was too late to turn back.

The inertia of my intentions had finally taken physical form, and I was finally going to produce the definitive answer I'd been seeking since I'd first seen my father's face on TV nearly five years ago. It had taken so much courage to get here, and I really hoped he would accept me. I'd prayed for so much more than having him simply write me a check before writing me out of his life. But either way, I told myself I had nothing to lose.

I ran up the back stairs to Henry's office and removed my baseball cap and fixed my hair with a quick sweep of my hand before walking in, trying to look much more collected than I was.

Mom was already there, looking beautiful and ready to go into battle, too. Today, the world and my father would finally get to meet the successful woman she was today, not the scared young woman who had let him control her seventeen years ago. Today she would try to clear her name, and I would try to claim mine.

Henry came to take me back to his office in order to prep me before facing the press. He explained that he'd address the cameras first with a prepared statement detailing our legal claims against the Governor, then he'd turn it over to me to answer questions from the press. "Just tell the truth, you'll do great."

Henry walked into the conference room first, followed by Mom and me. I stood tall and walked with purpose, aware the cameras were rolling. I couldn't believe how many reporters there were. I looked out into the sea of lenses that seemed to go on forever, even extending out into the hallway on the other side of the room, the flashbulbs going off like a fireworks finale.

Breathe Kara, just breathe, and try to look happy. My defensive perma-smile went up as we sat down on either side of Henry, who was standing in front of a bouquet of microphones.

More flashbulbs.

"This morning, at approximately 10:00 a.m., a complaint for Filiation was filed by my client, Kara Hewes, against Bruce Sundlun, presently the Governor of Rhode Island."

"Based on a blood test voluntarily submitted by the Governor and his daughter, Kara, we have definitive proof that Bruce Sundlun is the father of Kara Hewes. Kara has been trying for more than a year to have Bruce Sundlun admit that he is her legal father and assist her with day-to-day expenses. He offered to help her get into college and pay the magnificent sum of 1,000 a year."

Ouch, did he really need to say that?

I felt the sting of shame when Henry told the world about my father's cheap offer, something I had never shared with my friends, since I was so embarrassed. My father's insignificant offer had reinforced my deep-seated feelings of being less than, defective, and unworthy.

I kept my game face on, refusing to let the media capture my fears on camera as Henry expressed his anger.

"We understand that Governor Sundlun is a man of great means, but that isn't the sole criterion. His income is not the essential part of this action. We need validation that he is her father."

Yes, I need that, really need that, more than anything.

"This case was started out of frustration caused by the Governor's absolute refusal to engage in meaningful settlement discussions regarding his daughter. It's unfortunate that he has embarrassed her by making her go public to prove her parentage."

Yes, he shamed me, and now everyone knew. Would they all think I was unworthy, too?

Henry then introduced me to the press. "Now I'd like to introduce Kara, and she can take some of your questions."

Oh God, it's my turn now. After all the years of theater and debate, I wasn't afraid to speak in public, but today I was playing the role of me, and I was afraid to say something wrong.

I took a gulp of air and hoped my voice wouldn't get high and squeaky from the tension in my throat.

More flashbulbs.

Speak slowly, I reminded myself as the questions darted at me like a ping pong ball.

"What do you want the Governor to do?"

"I'd like him to be a father."

At least the reporters seemed to be treating me with kid gloves.

"Can you afford to go to college without his support?"

"I'm not destitute, but he's my father, and he should do the right thing. I want to get to know him, and I want him to accept me, just like all of his other children."

"Where do you want to go to school?" a reporter asked.

"I have been accepted to the University of Michigan and Boston University. I would have liked to go to Boston, but I can't afford the private tuition. I applied there because I thought it would be nice to be closer to my father, so we could start getting to know each other."

My eyes darted over at Mom, to see her expression about the possibility of going east.

"Judy, the Governor claims you are just after his money. Is that true?"

"No, of course not. I'm not asking for anything. I just can't see how he can be that tough to not see his daughter, and realize how lucky he is."

Thanks, Mom, for always believing in me, even when you're mad.

"Kara, what do you think of how the Governor is treating your mother?"

I could kill him. "I have no respect for him when he does that. She has done nothing but keep me in our home and make sure I had everything I need."

I looked at Mom, hoping she could feel me standing up for her. She had survived raising me alone, and now I felt like I needed to protect her. Our roles were often reversed, but she'd made me who I was. My strength came, in part, because she'd leaned on me.

I took a few more questions before Henry brought things to a close. "Okay, ladies and gentlemen, thank you for coming. Kara and her mother are going to go home and rest now. You all have copies of the lawsuit to refer to. Thank you."

When it was over, I couldn't wait to find the girls waiting for me in Henry's office. I had invited Brooke and Dayna, and a few more of my close friends to attend the news conference for moral support, and to witness what was going to be the biggest moment of my life. I had attended their Bat Mitzvah parties, sweet sixteen parties, and dance recitals — this was my coming out party.

I gave them a huge hug of relief. "Thank you for coming!"

"Of course, we would be here. You were great, so great!" Dayna said.

"So amazing," Brooke echoed, "Were you nervous?"

"A little," I confessed.

We finished our hugs and went looking for the juice and Danish Henry had put out. There were a couple of newspaper photographers allowed back in the office, and my friends and I posed, linking arm and arm for pictures.

The next day, I sat on the floor of our apartment reading the newspapers. Some of my favorite articles were the ones showing me with all of my friends. It felt special to stand with the closest thing I had to sisters and show the world I had a father.

Many of the papers wrote about the "striking resemblance" between the Governor and me, putting our photos side by side for people to compare.

The Detroit Free Press headline said: "Accept me," Kara Hewes fights for her name...

The New York Times wrote: Paternity Suit Just Another Crisis in Rhode Island.

Sidebar stories quoted experts who analyzed what emotional issues I must have and why I had to do this. "Sundlun's absence in her childhood and his reluctance to acknowledge her were bound to inflict pain and anger."

I didn't want my wounds laid out like a test case for the world to see, that my life was somehow an example of what can happen when a father screws up. I was hoping they weren't right. I didn't want to think I was that screwed up, and I didn't want anyone else to look at me that way, either.

The expert went on to say, "Anger is about hurt...you have to ask, what does she really want?"

The expert was right; I wanted him to accept me, to love me, to do the right thing, so I wouldn't look like a rejected fool in front of the whole world. I wanted to not be so angry. It was a feeling I had known for as long as I could remember. Growing up, I unleashed it on Mom, but I know good and well that part of that furor came from his rejection. There was a tear in my soul and it had ached my whole life, and only he could stitch it.

"The Sundlun case exploded because it's been kept under wraps for so long. The person who breaks out, breaks the secret, wants to say, 'This is who I am. I am the daughter of Bruce Sundlun.' We don't search to hurt, we search to heal," reported *The Providence Journal*.

Yes, I needed him to heal me and give me my place in the world, but I didn't like seeing it in the paper because it made me feel way too vulnerable. The reporters kept calling me a celebrity, and a part of me appreciated the recognition. It wasn't the same as the validation of a father, but it felt good to finally have this out in the open, especially since most of the stories were sympathetic. "He's a pretty important man, so he should do the right thing," said Marc, a college student in Rhode Island. "She wants a dad, he's being cold blooded."

Other comments hurt and touched that dark place of
unworthiness that I tried to block out. "It seems like an eleventh
hour try for money," said Barbara in Warwick.

The media helped me communicate what I so badly needed
to say to my father, and this time he was forced to listen. He
could no longer put me off; he would be forced to act. I wouldn't
have to wonder if he got my letters or understood me. It was all
there in black and white.

The next night, my father came back with his own message
in an exclusive interview on Channel 10, the NBC station in
Providence that he used to run before he ran for governor.

I caught the broadcast on our local Detroit news. Sitting on
the floor of our apartment, I stared at the TV as he spoke about
me. He wore his trademark double breasted suit and striped tie
as he looked in the camera and started to speak in his deep
voice. "The Kara in that news conference was not the same girl I
met last year. She's been coached, manipulated by her lawyer
and mother."

*No, I haven't, I'm just showing my tough side — the side I
inherited from you. And I wouldn't have had to do any of this if you'd
just done the right thing.*

I was dumbfounded. More to the point, he was making me
mad. He didn't seem like the nice guy I'd met, either.

Then he directed his message directly to me. "It's going to
be difficult, but somehow or another, you and I have got to fight
our way through those obstructions. We've got to get by Mr.
Baskin, we've got to get by your mother. My hands are out and
my heart is open. I hope yours is, too."

*What? Isn't that what I've been trying to do since I wrote you my
first letter, met you in secret, passed a DNA test, and then finally filed
a lawsuit after you kept ignoring my pleas?*

Then he went back to addressing the camera. "I really don't
think I can be accused of ignoring Kara, or not wanting to have a
relationship with her. Candidly, I don't feel the same way about
Judith Hewes."

Don't you dare go there again!

I felt an angry, defensive flame rise in my gut, and the fire in me was starting to rage. *Of course*, he had been ignoring me! Who's he kidding? And why does he have to take cheap shots at my mother? Doesn't he know he hurts me by doing that?

As angry as I was and as little sense as it made, my heart was grasping at the one ray of light: "My heart is open, and my hands are out."

That was the part of him I'd felt when I met him, the part that had cemented my faith, the part that made this quest seem not as crazy as it sounded.

But could I really trust him, or was it all just wishful thinking? Was I crazy? Then again, I had nothing to lose and everything to gain.

Clearly, the media firestorm was forcing him to rethink his position, but part of me didn't care. Was it possible for people to change? To realize they've been wrong? Baskin was suspicious. So was Mom, who wasted no time expressing her opinion. "Sure, now he responds. He's just trying to save himself, since the public sees how bad he's been."

Mom was boiling mad, and I couldn't blame her. She had no reason to have any faith in him, and, unlike me, nothing to gain.

"I'm the one who raised you all alone, and all he can do is slander me. What kind man does that?"

"Maybe he'll make things right if we just give him a chance." I could hope, couldn't I?

"He better apologize to me and issue a retraction for his slur campaign, or I'm going to have to sue him for damages because he's trying hurt my business."

She raged on, then calmed down and apologized for getting angry. "You should do what you want, and I'll support you."

Mom was built soft and sensitive, and got her feelings easily hurt on a good day. I worried what this might do to her and our relationship. I didn't want to gain a father at the expense of losing my mother. But I knew as much as this hurt, her love was unconditional. Unfortunately, I had no control over the media monster that was growing.

It had been a crazy week, and my patience and heart were on emotional overload. My father's news conference had been on Tuesday, mine was Wednesday, and now on Thursday, he was making his television appeal.

Henry said he would be in contact with my father's lawyers over the weekend to try and reach a settlement. In the meantime, he asked that we not do anything more on our own with the press. Technically, the law wasn't on our side, since Mom had signed the settlement papers years ago. But Henry hoped the public pressure would force my father to settle again.

Today, what happened to me would be illegal. We can thank the famous basketball player Isiah Thomas, who tried to give the mother of his child a lump sum. The courts ruled that parents must provide for the child over the course of his or her lifetime.

But in 1993, my case was a lightning rod, in part because I was a teen fighting for my own rights, since Mom had given hers up. All weekend long, the press was camped outside my house, my school, and anywhere else they thought they might find someone who knew me. As a reporter now, I know they were all looking for the M-O-S sound bite, or Man-On-the-Street, interview they could use in their live reports that night. And this brought out some pretenders.

One TV news reporter asked a girl in my class at the 7-11 what she thought. "Shocking, just shocking. Kara never talked about it."

Of course, I didn't. I'd barely spoken two words to the girl.

The Providence Journal called it a "secret rarely shared," quoting my classmate, Jerry, who probably said it best: "This was a shock to a lot of her friends. I don't think a lot of people expected her dad to be a governor of a state, and a millionaire."

Brooke, who had been through it all with me, said, "She told her close, close friends...she didn't want to make a big deal of it."

Thankfully, school was already out, so I didn't have to walk past news cameras on my way to class. But that didn't stop the news crews from using West Bloomfield High as a backdrop for their reports. I tried to go about my normal days, but now when my boyfriend picked me up, he ended up on the front page of the paper driving me away in his convertible.

Though Henry had asked me not to give any interviews, I did give my baby picture to Barbara Meagher, a TV reporter from WLNE the then-CBS station in Providence, who had been camped outside for a while. Where most reporters just raised their cameras to start taking pictures when I walked by, Barbara showed a human, almost maternal, side and asked how I was holding up without shoving a camera in my face. She kindly asked if she could have a baby picture to show on the news that night. I gave it to her because she was so nice, and promised not to ask me any questions. I will never forget how gracious and sympathetic she was, a rare commodity when compared to the other reporters. I also hoped my father would see my baby picture on the news.

Inside Edition and *Hard Copy* were both offering to pay for my interview, but Henry advised against my granting either offer. "You may get ten grand, but that won't help you form a relationship with your dad, which is what you really want."

He was right, but I was really sad to turn down Oprah. She wasn't offering money, but I was dying to meet her. There was one national interview Henry thought would be good for us to do, so he set up a time for *People Magazine* to photograph and interview me at his house. I was so young and put all my trust in Henry. So far, he'd been right about everything. But the *People Magazine* article was not my favorite. I wanted the article to help me appeal to my father's heart. Instead, they slammed him.

It was a sunny day, so we took the pictures out on Henry's beautiful deck. I tried to smile and give upbeat answers, show my optimism that everything would work out. I couldn't wait for the magazine to hit the stands to see what they wrote.

When I opened up my issue with Burt Reynolds and Loni Anderson on the cover, I felt a sinking disappointment.

They labeled me the Gov Child, and used black and white shots that seemed to convey sadness. They'd made Henry's pretty deck look more like a boxing ring. The article criticized my father for leaving the TV on when we met for the first time, calling him cold, even though I'd told them I didn't mind. They interviewed his ex-wives on his "aloof" approach to parenting, all agreeing that his career was always a priority.

"He wasn't around that much," said his first wife, Madeleine Gimbel. "He wasn't involved with the children." Wife No. 3, Joy Sundlun, added, "Bruce is Bruce. He was very much a businessman."

It's not that I couldn't see my father was playing hardball, but rather, I knew there was something under his game. I held on to the television appeal he'd personally made to me about how his heart was open, and hoped this article wouldn't make him change his mind. Actually, Henry's strategy worked, and the excessive press coverage apparently put enough pressure on my father to come up with a settlement offer by Monday. More than a year of battling in secret was resolved in six intense days with a very public offer to do much more than just pay me off.

My father's attorney told Henry he wanted to settle the lawsuit right away and begin to "get to know me." He promised to pay for tuition at the University of Michigan and, beyond that, treat me as he would any of his other children. Then he did something that shocked everyone: Not only would he pay for all of my college expenses, but he invited me to move out to Rhode Island for the summer to live with him so we could, "get to know each other."

Leapin' lizards! I really do feel like Annie. What did he just say? *Get to know each other?* I had dreamed of this moment for so long, and it was hard to believe it was finally here. The fairy tale had grown wings, and was now about to soar. Could I really go live with him in his castle and live happily ever after? It all seemed too good to be true. Could he really love me the way I wanted him to? Did he really want to try? Why did he change his mind?

I would later learn his offer even surprised his staff, who had no idea he was going to come around that much. He was a man who kept his thoughts close to the vest until he was ready to announce a battle plan. One might think it was politically expedient to make the scandal go away—and it was—but my father never cared about being politically correct. He liked to shoot first and ask questions later—literally.

To prove the point, earlier that year, he had shot raccoons in his yard and, instead of keeping it quiet, he walked into the state police to turn himself in. The press had a field day with a sitting governor accused of illegally shooting off guns at his estate, but my father said he would have done it all over again, since they were trying to hurt a baby fox and he just couldn't allow that. Eventually, the charges were dropped, but the comics still featured raccoons with GOP buttons.

Patti would later tell me it was clear to her he was smitten with me and wanted to try to be a father. She said she could tell by the way his face lit up when he talked about me. She later joked that I should have just told them I straightened my hair, then he wouldn't have needed a DNA test, since he had a standing appointment at the barber shop to chemically smooth his curls.

Henry beamed. "This is it, kid, this is what you have wanted."

I hadn't realized how tightly wound I'd been until I felt huge weights lift off my shoulders. The validation I'd so badly needed was already rebuilding my core. The effects of a sudden new reality were overwhelming. I was elated, yet I also worried about Mom.

I wanted to jump up and down and scream a victory whoop, and yell from the top of the mountains, "We did it! He's accepting me as his daughter!" But I had to think about Mom. She'd always said she wanted me to know him, but I don't think she ever wanted me to go *live* with him. And no one could have ever expected he'd extend an invitation. Sometimes her fear of losing me bubbled over with statements she would always regret later. "You just want to be with him because he's rich and famous. He never wanted us, you know. I was the one who raised you all alone."

I couldn't deny that my father's fame and power was exciting to me, but it wasn't why I wanted him in my life. I wanted a father, plain and simple. But the fact that mine came with a fairytale mansion and the stature of a king made me feel like a princess getting rescued. I was elated the DNA fit but, unlike Cinderella, my mom wasn't wicked, and I desperately wished there could be a fairy-something to magically change her life, too. I felt as though I was being torn in half and forced to choose one over the other, and it was impossible to do. Instead, I had to follow my heart, which meant leaving Mom alone in the scary forest while I went to live in the castle with the man she was starting to hate all over again.

There would be no vindication for her. Though she had filed a defamation lawsuit against him, nothing came of it. My father refused to apologize, and reiterated that he was only going to help me. The laws back then weren't fair, but the script had been written. She had signed the settlement back when I was a baby, so she had no legal footing. Instead, she would play the role of victim, thus refueling my inner turmoil that tore at me every day. Painted as the golden child, I lived between guilt and elation, and my emotions pixilated like a kaleidoscope. Despite my angst, I never doubted I would be leaving everything I knew to go live with him. Entering into the unknown, I would accept his offer of acceptance.

9 Guess Who's Coming to Dinner?

Wednesday, June 16, 1993

Whisked from my suburban apartment for the land of sailboats and mansions, I was ready to start my new life with my father, where people still had debutante parties and wore black ties on a regular basis. After all the media storm and requests for interviews, I'd felt like an extra appendage. The attorneys had done the deal making, and I'd had only a brief, awkward telephone conversation with my father in Henry's office after we made a verbal agreement to drop the paternity suit.

"Hi, so I guess I'll be coming to spend some time with you this summer. I'm excited. It'll be great." So much for memorable or clever.

"We are looking forward to having you at Seaward," my father answered formally. "Newport is a wonderful place, and you will enjoy it."

"Um, okay, I love the beach."

"We have beautiful beaches here."

"Great. Well thanks so much for everything you are doing for me. I'll see you soon," I said in my sweetest voice, trying to show him I still was the girl he'd liked.

"Ok, 'bye."

Obviously, it had been easier for both of us to communicate through our attorneys, but we no longer had them as our safety net, and we'd have to learn how to talk to each other—especially if I was going to live with him.

How I wished my attorney could handle the communication problems I was now having with Mom. My whole life, she had always loved to tell me about my father's world. Now that I was getting ready to leave her for the life she'd talked about for so long, I'm sure this wasn't exactly her fantasy ending. Her reasoning was that she'd done all the hard work of raising me only to give me, her crown jewel, away to a man who, instead of being remorseful or even grateful, was rejecting her once again.

Mom was a bundle of opposites. She would say how happy she was for me one moment, then lash out the next, furious that the olive branch was only being extended to me. Since he wouldn't speak to her, I was the only one she could yell at, and the fact she thought I looked and acted like him made me even more of a target. The furrow between my brows, the shape of my mouth, and my curly hair were all physical triggers for what seemed like post-traumatic stress disorder.

"I raised you alone, so don't you think your mother deserves something?

"Of course I do, but I'm seventeen, what can I do?"

"Shouldn't you fight for your mother?"

"How?"

"Don't you care that he destroyed me?"

I felt like putting my hands over my ears. *He didn't destroy you, it will all be okay, please stop yelling at me.* I had to retreat because challenging her anger only made it grow.

I wished I could call my father and ask him to please stop being a jerk to Mom and apologize...preferably on TV, so her friends could hear. Couldn't he just say how happy he is that she raised his daughter? Couldn't he give her some money to help her out after all she did for him? I wanted him to rescue both of us, not just me, and I worried that taking his lifeboat meant Mom would be left to drown. I thought of Brooke's quote in the paper: "Kara and her mom are like crutches for each other." What will happen when I'm not there to hold her up? I was too new to the job of being a man's daughter, and I couldn't tell him my thoughts. So I said nothing to him about Mom.

Mom had always taught me to be grateful for any blessing. My father's desire to finally accept me was the blessing I'd been praying for, yet he was also the curse that was breaking my mother's heart.

Looking back, I know she was terrified of losing me. I was all she had. Of course, I had room for two parents in my heart, but proving that to Mom was becoming difficult in the face of her insecurities and anger, which created a wall between us. I understood her pain, but I couldn't take it on; it was too heavy, and I felt like it would pull me under. I couldn't repay the debts of my father's wrongs. As hard as I know it was, Mom agreed to drop her lawsuit accusing him of slander, so I could move on with my life. But she couldn't let go of the hurts, and they multiplied within her, hardening her heart. It seemed ironic that after everything I'd been through, my father was opening, and she was closing down. She remained determined to dig her heels in until she got some kind of retribution, something I feared would never come. And it was ripping me apart.

Would it be better to stay and refuse to settle until he apologized to Mom? I didn't think so, and I didn't want to be bait. Her rage made me feel guilty for getting the better deal, and I felt equally ashamed about looking forward to leaving the toxic environment of our apartment. To lessen my inner turmoil, I told myself college would start in the fall, and Mom would have to adjust to me leaving anyway. But the reality was that it felt like I had just gained a father and lost my mom. She would be left behind to read all about my new adventures, and all I could do is promise to call a lot. I hoped she'd soften over time.

On June 16, 1993, exactly one month before my eighteenth birthday, and seven days after filing my lawsuit, I left West Bloomfield, Michigan to begin the next chapter of my life. I couldn't wait to get to meet my father and my new family. This time, my meeting with my father would be anything but secret. The press was invited to dinner and a news conference to get one last story before we signed a gag order and requested our privacy. I was only going for one night, then I'd return back home to pack my things and say goodbye to Mom.

I raced up I-275 to Detroit Metro Airport, where I met Henry at the gate. He was accompanying me to Rhode Island to witness my signing of the papers affirming that my paternity suit would be dropped. Henry wasn't the only one waiting for me. The press had guessed which plane I was on, and were waiting with microphones ready to launch.

"Kara, are you excited to go meet your dad?" a reporter yelled extending the microphone in front of my face.

"Are you happy it's over?"

"Did you get what you wanted?"

Uh oh, I wasn't expecting this. "Yes, I'm thrilled to begin the process of building a father-daughter relationship, and I look forward to getting to know my other family tonight."

Henry bolted toward us, saving the day. "Thank you all, but we have to get Kara on board right now. We'll see you all tomorrow."

"Sorry, I'm late," I murmured.

"Let's go, kid, they're about to close the jetway."

The stewardess shot me a disapproving look as I passed by and sank down into my seat. The sudden press gauntlet made my insides unravel. Thankfully, I had a little over an hour to decompress before we landed in Providence.

"There will probably be more press on the other end," Henry said, "so keep being you. This is such a great story. They love you, and you deserve this, kiddo. People love a happy ending."

When we landed at T.F. Green airport about an hour later, there was a state police cruiser waiting for us on the tarmac. I walked down the stairs to the runway, aware the trooper was nervous as he scanned the tarmac for press. This was my father's way of making sure we didn't make any news before the planned dinner that night.

Mission accomplished, the trooper drove us away without one flashbulb going off. The papers would later report how the reporters inside the airport were duped. Henry would be equally hard to find because he checked into a hotel under a different name. It seemed daunting to go on without him, since he'd been with me the whole way. But he told me he'd meet me at the State House in the morning to sign the papers before the news conference. "Don't be late this time," he joked.

"I won't!"

As the state trooper drove me to my father's home, I wondered what it looked like. Butterflies were dancing in my stomach, but for once it was the good kind of nervous—the kind that acknowledged how hard I'd fought for this day, and that I was finally ready to take my place at the table.

A half-hour later, we entered the charming town of Newport. Colonial houses lined the streets, looking so perfect it appeared straight out of a movie set. The ocean, tinged with green, gave off a more pungent smell than the beaches I'd seen in places like Florida. We turned on Cliff Avenue and entered through two stately brick columns marked "Private Way," where the road became gravel. I caught glimpses of the ocean in between the driveways of the expansive waterfront estates.

I had never seen houses with names before, let alone two entrances—one for service, and the other for the main house—and I wondered if I needed to click my heels and whisper, "There's no place like home." The car slowed as we approached the "Seaward" sign at the end of my father's driveway. We turned left onto a dirt driveway circling a glorious old tree that stood taller than the two-story stucco house. The car stopped in front of the double doors where my father was waiting. Wearing a warm smile, he opened my door and extended his hand. He didn't let go as we walked toward the house. It felt strange to hold his hand, but I loved resting mine in his as we stopped to share a joint smile for the cameras. Even though I was aware of being on stage, I wasn't nervous or scared this time. Nope, this time the huge Cheshire cat grin spread across my face matched what my heart was feeling. The fact that my father looked equally happy made it all the more surreal.

Thankfully, this was a photo op only, and the press was not allowed to ask any questions. But I don't think they went away disappointed. Here we were at long last, me, my father…and his assistant, Patti, who was standing in the wings, smiling in a pink suit, ready to join us as we climbed the steps where my father opened the tall double doors for me to enter the large foyer of his home. The cameras went wild as I smiled and walked across the threshold of my new life. Pictures of my father escorting me into his estate to meet my new family were the money shot that would cycle on TV and lead newspaper articles for days to come. TV had come full circle for me. It had helped me find my father, made him accept me, and now would bear witness to the reunion.

I was led into the living room where French doors opened onto a patio overlooking acres of green lawn that stretched out to the famous Cliff Walk. The panoramic view of the ocean took my breath away, and the moist air made me feel as if I could float. Should I pinch myself to make sure this isn't a dream? Wow, was I really going to live here?

My father broke into my thoughts. "This is my wife, Marjorie."

"Hello, Hello!" she said rushing toward me.

Marjorie was exuberant and warm, and greeted me with a big hug. I had been told her accident left her with severe brain damage, but I couldn't tell. She invited us to sit down on couches covered in white silken flowered fabric. I tried to not sink into the soft cushions, while the press took pictures of us smiling, happy to become a "family." After a half-hour, my father's press people decided the media had gotten enough, and they were escorted out.

Marjorie led me into the formal dining room that had a commanding view of the ocean. Again, I found myself forcing the air into my lungs. Such beauty! Place cards adorned the elegant, long table filling the room. I couldn't believe this was my father's home—with its sheer perfection, it looked more like a hotel. Do I really have an unlimited stay? It was hard not to feel dizzy. For so long, I had envied my friend's beautiful homes, but nothing had prepared me for this. I wondered whose names were on the place cards and how I was related to them. As it turned out, they were Marjorie's grown children, Mark and Kim, and Kim's husband, Chris.

Marjorie's warm welcome made me feel better about moving into her home for the summer. She seemed genuinely excited to meet me, and despite her short term memory problems that sometimes made her repeat herself, she operated like the graceful First Lady she was by welcoming me to her dinner table and introducing me to her children. Mark, in his early twenties, reminded me of Tom Cruise, with his chiseled jaw, dark hair, and athletic physique. He lived at Seaward and promised to show me around Newport. While he seemed sincerely happy to meet me, Kim was just the opposite. She resembled Mark with her pretty, big eyes and dark hair, but remained completely silent until about halfway through dinner, when she started sobbing. It took me a moment to realize the tears were because of me. I didn't know what to say, so I just looked down at my plate hoping to pick up the right fork. Were we just going to let her cry it out? Everyone seemed to be ignoring her tantrum, so I just tried my best to blend.

"Would you like some more vegetables?" the server asked me.

"No thank you, I'm okay."

Each time I spoke, Kim's crying intensified. It appeared as though the very sound of my voice touched the part in her that screamed, *Why does SHE have to be here?*

I'm not sure when he left, but I just remember looking up from my plate and noticing my father was no longer at the table. He had gone to take a call in the other room, and in his absence her wall of composure collapsed, and she stared to wail.

I didn't know what to do, and neither did her husband, Chris. It couldn't have been easy, and my heart went out to him. He attempted to comfort his wife while being mindful of the importance of this dinner and the awkwardness that was building. It became clear Kim wasn't going to regain her composure, so Chris stood up and helped her away from the table. "I'm going to take her home, it's just a bit much for her."

The press had gone and my fairytale evening at the mansion become strangely Kafkaesque, complete with someone sobbing at the table. I was exasperated and, well, a little angry. I had fought hard for my place at the table, and her hysterics tarnished what was supposed to be a big night in my life. But I hid my hurt and smiled through it all.

I thought once I won over my father, everything would be perfect, but I was quickly learning it wasn't going to be that easy. Just because my father decided to accept me, didn't mean everyone else had to. All I'd ever wanted was a father, and I hadn't realized how my presence would affect so many people. I had imagined our relationship in a vacuum, and was now realizing I would not only have to get to know him, but learn the rules of a whole new family dynamic. "I hope she feels better," I said, as if my surfacing was something she could sleep off.

After they left, Mark tried to smooth things over. "It's not your fault. This is just hard for her." He explained how the two of them didn't have a good relationship with their biological father, and my father had become their true father figure. Kim felt like she was being replaced by a "real" daughter. Ironic how my "real" father filled *their* void, while creating mine. I felt for her, and hoped she wouldn't see me as the enemy.

We never spoke again about that night. That summer she would come over from time to time with her young children to use the trampoline, but I always had the feeling she believed she got bounced for me. My entry into my father's life forever changed hers, and while he built a game changing relationship with me, she was sidelined as the forgotten step-sister. It probably wasn't fair, and I felt for Kim, but I couldn't shoulder the blame for my father never telling anyone about me.

Unlike Kim, Mark couldn't have been friendlier, that night after all the formalities were over, he offered to take me out so I could see the town. I welcomed the chance to let down my hair and hang out with someone near my age who knew all the ins and outs of this new world I had entered. The press was still loitering about outside, so I got in the back of his car while he piled blankets on top of me so they wouldn't see me. We laughed hysterically about pulling off our escape for some hot cocoa. Chocolate always helped me feel better, and I was relieved to know someone sweet would be living with me in my father's house for the summer.

The rest of that night was a blur after Kim's departure. Looking back now, I'm not even sure if I said goodnight to my father, since the evening had been more about getting to know him through the people with whom he shared his life. The unreality of it all was a lot to take in—the cameras, the sobbing —but I knew I needed to keep performing. Like Cinderella, I had managed to make it to the ball, but feared my chariot could still turn into a pumpkin if I didn't curtsy right. Looking back, my father's lack of response to the drama at his dinner table could have seemed cold and aloof, but I saw it as strength. With the emotion as thick as pea soup in the room, he'd weathered the storm without so much as a comment. His decision to bring me into his home had been made, and no one was going to sway him. He was just the kind of rock I needed to make me feel safe, and I admired his ability to stay strong in a storm.

Mom had always told me I was wired like him—his emotions came with a hold button; something that didn't come on Mom's model. I used my hold button that day, and I have used it countless times since in my career as a TV journalist, especially when breaking horrible news to the public as a newscaster. In retrospect, I know my father and I were using our "hold buttons" as we tried to survive each moment of scrutiny in the early days of our relationship. We both shared the same survival instinct that allowed us to detach from emotions before they buried us, and we digested the stress moment by moment. Just like when he ran from church to church to escape the Nazis and stay alive, I knew I had to keep making it through each challenge to keep alive my dream of having a father.

That night I went to sleep in the "green" room—all of the guest rooms were named after the color of their décor—and as I snuggled under the fine sheets, I fell asleep feeling excited and optimistic. I'd begun walking down a whole new road—one that included my father. Soon I would get to meet my half-brothers, and I hoped we would get along as well as I did with Mark. Tomorrow they could watch me on TV when my father and I faced the press together for the first time to announce I was dropping my lawsuit. I closed my eyes, telling myself there would be plenty of time to really get to know each other once the show was over.

10 We Now Pronounce You Father and Daughter

The next morning my father and I met in the kitchen and ate some eggs and toast Mrs. Schuster, the housekeeper, made for us. We needed to fuel up for our big day in front of the media where, for the first time together, we'd make a public pledge to become a real father and daughter. I thought he looked handsome in his trademark double breasted suit and striped tie, and was thrilled that he liked my black suit.

"You look very nice," he said in a chipper voice. It was obvious he was raring to go.

"Thank you," I answered, feeling excited as well.

"Let's go, we don't want to be late." The trooper stood to attention, and we all went out to his cruiser to begin the forty-five minute ride from Seaward to the State House.

I looked forward to riding alone with my father to the State House. With all the whirlwind swirling about, I needed the quiet of the car to get mentally ready. As we pulled into the State House, a sea of reporters was there to capture my father opening the door for me and helping me out of the car. The cameras went wild as my father reached out in a protective way to grab my hand to walk up the steps to the State House, both of us wearing wide smiles…and this time my smile wasn't plastered on my face as a protective mask to what was in my heart. I was truly happy. My father seemed larger than life, tall, confident, and ready to take on any reporter. We went up several flights of stairs, until we got to the door with the gold letters that said "Governor's Office."

While the reporters and TV cameras waited to "take us live" from the State House, my father and I met in his private office and signed an out of court settlement. He agreed to pay all of my college expenses. Beyond that, he said he would like to treat me like any of his other children, which was priceless. DNA and legalities proved I was his daughter, but now I had hope of becoming his daughter in his heart.

While I embraced finding the other half of me, the media weighed in with their own opinions. Some legal analysts quipped in the newspapers that he was getting off easy, arguing that my father should use his millions to pay my mother back child support and guarantee me an inheritance in his will. One article entitled "Why Kara Wants More," added up how much boarding school, equestrian lessons, and trips around the world would have cost, given this is how my brothers grew up.

A financial windfall would have been nice, and I do think my mother deserved more, but this agreement had something money couldn't buy. It expressed his intention to *be* a father to me, that when and if he helped me do more, it would be because he wanted to, not because he was ordered to.

I had a few moments to prepare before facing the cameras, so I slipped into my father's private bathroom to brush my hair. When I came out a jovial man startled me when he reached out his hand and said, "Hi, I'm your cousin Fenton!" He was clearly excited to meet me.

My father chimed in, "We call him Nepotism around here. He's a travel agent and always wants to book my trips!"

Though I could see some facial similarities, these two men couldn't have been more opposite. Fenton was as skinny as they come, dressed in khakis and a button down shirt which, he informed me, was his idea of dressing up. "Even if I don't book your father's trips, I do pretty well booking Spring Break trips for the students at Brown University. Hey, you'll have to come to one of the parties on campus with me," he said, reminding me of the frat boy who never grew up.

He was younger than my father, for sure, but I couldn't tell how much. I later learned he kept his age a carefully guarded secret. I think it was his way of making sure he could act like a kid and get away with it.

"This is so cool — it's just so cool that Bruce has a daughter," he said while looking at my father and shaking his head in amazement.

Dad looked at his watch and patted Fenton on the back. "Okay, we'll have to hold this until later. Time to go."

It was thrilling to meet members of my new family, especially one so outgoing and friendly. After Kim's bolting from dinner the night before, I was worried about others' reactions to me. Fenton made those worries melt away. "Nice to meet you, Fenton."

My father and I left his office and walked toward the State Room, where all of the reporters were waiting. Photographers and TV cameras followed our every step as my father escorted me across the rich jewel-toned rug to the podium.

He stood tall behind the podium and addressed the media with a written statement. "Kara spent an evening at my home in Newport last evening, and we enjoyed a night together as she got to know my family."

He went on to say how he would pay for my college and looked forward to building a relationship with me when I moved into his home this summer.

Next, I read from the statement that a staffer had written for me. "I enjoyed meeting the family last night, and I look forward to coming back to spend some time in Newport before going off to college."

Once we were done with the script, the real fun started. My father used his charisma like a sword to cut through the tension in the room, jabbing back at each question they yelled out.

A reporter asked him how having a daughter would change him, and my father put on a big grin and quipped, "I assume I'll be getting more than the usual amount of Father's Day cards this year."

Everyone laughed. Given the varying opinions about our situation, his comment was the perfect icebreaker to what could have been a tense press conference.

When M. Charles Bakst, the legendary political columnist for the *Providence Journal*, started to ask me about my feelings toward my father's religion, my father interjected by turning to me and asking, "Do you know I'm Jewish?"

"Yes," I said with a nod.

More laughter.

"Good, next question," he said.

When they asked me what I wanted to be when I grew up, I said a television news reporter or a lawyer. Given the media firestorm my father had just emerged from, a reporter sarcastically asked my father if he wanted one of his children to become a member of the media.

"As long as she doesn't become a political columnist like Charlie, I'm okay." More laughter.

"Governor, do you think she inherited her interests in broadcasting and law from you?"

Mom never knew that after my father left Executive Jet and before he became governor, he was the CEO of the Outlet Corporation, one of the largest broadcasting companies in America. He started with just one station in Providence, and by the time he was done, he'd expanded the company to nearly a dozen stations. He was a trailblazer in the very field I wanted to enter. I couldn't help but dream of the doors he could open.

"Kara is still young; we'll send her off to the University of Michigan, and let's see what she can do. I'm happy to help her."

"Governor, do you see a resemblance?" a reporter shouted.

"I only have sons, and the three of them certainly don't resemble this beautiful girl," he answered with his signature charm.

My face ached from smiling so much, the energy was light and fun, and I was having such a great time laughing with my father that I nearly forgot we were being broadcasted across the globe.

When they asked me what I thought of my father I said, looking up at him giggling, "I think you're like a milk toast."

He looked back at me, grinning, but unsure how to take my meaning.

They'd misunderstood. I didn't mean milquetoast, because anyone who knew my father knew he was far but bland, so I clarified things. "I mean you're hard on the outside and soft on the inside, like a cookie that softens in milk."

He belted out a deep laugh and gave me a pat on the back. "Okay then, whatever you say."

I was a softening agent for him. His warm heart had always been there, but having a daughter around somehow gave him permission to reveal it. Today when the newspapers run a picture on the anniversary of our story, they always show the one with my father and I laughing so hard it looks like I could have caught flies in my mouth. We were having the best time together, and I admired my father's honesty, even when the tough questions came.

"How will you make up for lost time, Governor?"

"Look, we can't wave a magic wand and create a relationship, but we are going to do this one day at a time."

He was right; there was no fairy godmother to erase the past, but it was clear the magic of the two of us coming together was a great new beginning—and who could ask for more than that?

My father ended the news conference by requesting the media give us some space. "We now ask for privacy, so we can start building a meaningful father-daughter relationship."

When it was over, I could tell Henry was pleased. "You were like a beacon of light; happy, calm, and you do look and speak just like him."

Life was good. I left with Henry to go back home to Michigan and pack for my big move.

Soon the cameras would depart and move on to the next scandal, leaving us to do the real work of building the relationship we both said we wanted.

In the final scene of *Annie*, Daddy Warbucks throws her a big party with elephants and fireworks on the lawn to celebrate their new life together, but they never show what happens after they go inside his big mansion to start their real life. The movie ends and we are all left to wonder. Would he become the father he promised to be? Would the excitement last when the cameras were gone? I would have to find out.

11 Hi Dad, I'm Home

I really did feel like Annie when I moved into the "Blue Room" in my father's Newport estate, and I knew I was going to like it there. Though I had slept in the "Green Room" for our family dinner, that was just for guests, and this was to be "my" room. Finally, a place to call my own that represented the new stature I had in my father's life. I must really be family if I get a room, right? I quietly closed the door and smiled to myself. Everything was so beautiful, it was hard to believe I was now going to live here. I made sure not to lay anything down on the crisp white bedspreads that covered the two twin beds for fear I might make a mark.

I carefully arranged my t-shirts and shorts in the drawers of the handsome mahogany antique dressers before moving into the bathroom attached to my room. It felt like a luxurious hotel suite. In keeping with the blue theme, there was a blue oversized square bathtub with matching blue flowers on the shower curtain. It was just calling to me to take a soak. All of the towels had a blue monogrammed "S" that the housekeeper, Mrs. Schuster, kept perfectly folded.

Again, I think I need to pinch myself.

Looking at all this luxury sent my nerves into overload. I didn't want to make any mistakes, so it was hard to relax. I felt like I was still performing.

I shouldn't have been nervous; Marjorie was sweet as pie and worked hard to make me feel at home, and Mark let me know I was invited to go to the beach with him and his friends anytime I wanted. But my father had other ideas.

As I came downstairs, he greeted me with a kind smile. "Kara, since I still have to run this state, I think the best way for us to get to know each other is if you just come with me. And you might learn something, too."

Though basking on the beach sounded great, I really wanted to soak up my father and get to know everything there was to know about him. And most importantly, I wanted to make up for lost time.

I felt like I needed to cram an entire childhood into one summer. I wanted to learn about him, and I hoped he wanted to find out more about me. Since my father was a man of action, our getting to know each other would come from doing, not talking.

"Sure, I'd love to go with you." I answered eagerly, without the slightest idea of what I'd be doing.

Each day was a new adventure, sometimes it was christening a submarine, other days it was shaking hands at a local veteran's potluck, I never knew what to expect, and it just added to the excitement.

One day we were walking on Narragansett town beach shaking hands when a woman asked him to kiss her baby. He happily obliged, then put his big strong arm around me. "Have you seen my new baby?" Then he kissed the top of my head.

The crowd roared with laughter, and so did we. Instead of trying to gloss over his huge mistakes, he was putting them out there front and center and owning them with humor. The laughter helped evaporate my long-held anger. I was having way too much fun to worry about the past. I kept reminding myself this was a new beginning, and to leave the past where it belongs. In the past.

It all could have been so awkward. I mean, how many teens meet their dad for the first time at seventeen? But thankfully, I felt innately at ease around him, and he brightened up around me. We just clicked, like two puzzle pieces that were always meant to be together. He was bringing me into his new world, and I loved the adventure…especially the night my father came home and asked me about a helicopter ride.

"Have you ever ridden in a helicopter?"

Definitely not a typical question I was used to getting. "Um, no."

"Well, tomorrow one is going to land in my yard, and you should be ready to go by 6 a.m." His smile told me he was proud to share a first with me. Imagine! A helicopter…landing on my father's back yard! No, Dorothy, you're definitely not in Kansas anymore.

I snapped him a sassy salute and snapped to attention. "Yes, sir!"

He had missed out on my first steps—my first lost tooth, my first school concert—but he'd definitely be there for this new milestone, and I was excited to share with him.

The truth is, when I was with him I always felt like I was flying. He was dashing, smart, and exciting, and listening to him talk was like reading an encyclopedia. He seemed to know everything about history, business, and the world in general. I was only seventeen, so I thought seventy-three was beyond ancient, but my father didn't seem old to me. Not only did he look much younger with his thick hair, smooth face, and strong physique, but his commanding energy was like a force of nature. Every time he entered a room, he seemed to change the very molecules in the air, and people wanted to get his attention. When he spoke to someone, he had a way of making them feel important, like they were the only one in the room. I loved the feeling of standing next to someone so magnetic, and thought he was the most exciting person I had ever met.

But living with my real-life Daddy Warbucks had its challenges, too. He was demanding and expected order and timeliness. He loved to tell me, "You can avoid almost any problem in life if you are on time and take care of your own equipment." —a rule he learned in the military.

I tried to keep up with the drills, but my habit of being late to everything was hard to break, and I was often running one step behind his warp speed.

He would often poke his head in my room with a hurried, "Are you ready, yet?"

"Almost," I would say, peeking my head out, trying to shield him from my messy equipment that included hair dryers, brushes, and make-up that littered my once-proper bathroom.

"Do you really need all that to get ready?" he would ask in disbelief, clearly new to the requirements of a teenage girl.

And I was new on the job of being a Governor's daughter, so sometimes I failed to get the orders right, like when my alarm didn't work and I awoke to the sounds of that helicopter outside.

Crap, he's going to kill me.

I raced around my room throwing on the same navy suit that had become my uniform for political events. I ran out to the chopper a bit disheveled and hoped he wouldn't notice. As I raced down the acres of lawn, I could see my father and the pilot waving their arms asking me to duck as I got closer to the chopper. I leaped in, and we were off to a long list of events.

I was learning my father was big on appearance, so I squirmed a bit when he looked at me strangely over his newspaper while sipping his coffee.

His eyes fixated on my wild bed-head. "Aren't you going to brush your hair?" *Think fast, Kara.* "Of course," trying to sound like I had it all figured out, "I just thought I'd wait until we were inside and away from the wind."

His arched eyebrow and slow smile let me know he knew good and well that I'd overslept. "Okay, whatever you say, dear."

Oops. Dad: 1, Kara: 0.

Just like he was changing my life, I was altering his. He was used to getting what he wanted with a snap of his finger, but I was not so snappy. He had brought home his new baby and was quickly figuring out his way of life wasn't going to work. And I was figuring out that giving him a big grin could ignite his patience.

Hair crisis averted!

As we flew over Rhode Island, it seemed like we were on top of the world, and he switched into paternal mode pointing out all the sites below and their history. I loved listening to his stories. The history lesson ended when the helicopter landed, and we switched into "there's lots of work to be done" mode.

After a crazy day of handshakes and photo ops, both my father and I were shaking in a different way. Just like me, he could get really crabby when he was hungry and needed some fuel.

"I'm starving, let's go get some dinner and ice cream. I know the perfect place."

"Great!" I was dying for food, too, and couldn't help but wonder if my blood sugar crashes came from him.

He took me to the Newport Creamery where we feasted on hamburgers and fries, knowing that the best part was coming…dessert. I had a wicked sweet tooth, and I discovered he did, too, when I noticed he never passed up a cookie or a donut at events.

When the waitress came by to take our ice cream orders, I almost fell out of the booth when he ordered a chocolate soda with chocolate ice cream! That had always been *my* drink! My friends used to make fun of me for my love of this retro bubbly concoction from another era, but I loved it and would order it at any old fashion ice cream parlor.

"I'll have the same thing," I said beaming. I looked at him and laughed. "Oh my gosh, that's so weird, that's what I always order. Maybe there's a chocolate gene?"

"You have great taste," he said smiling as he slurped down the soda, watching me do the same.

I was always scanning him for similarities, wondering quietly which parts of me came from him. But this was so obvious; we were instantly bonded over a love for chocolate.

We saw our reflections in this simple joy of sharing ice cream together. Of course, the helicopter was amazingly fun, but there was incredible comfort in the daily dose of love I had been craving for so long.

It was another stitch in the tapestry of our new father-daughter relationship, and with each special moment, we were weaving another connection.

As the days went on, I could tell my father really liked having me around. The troopers who drove him around would say things like, "He lights up when he's around you," and "Since you've been here, he's easier to get along with. Good thing you're a girl!"

Huh...Daddy Warbucks was softening.

Marjorie's accident made it difficult for her to attend so many events, so my father appointed me as his standing date, and as we grew closer, he started to make my roles more public.

"Kara, how would you like to march with me in the 4th of July parade in Bristol? It's world famous."

"That sounds amazing! I would love it!" It didn't matter that it was world famous—I was spending time with my father, and that was enough for me.

When the day came, I thought he would love the pleated navy skirt with white polka dots and a red stripe along the bottom. I paired it with a white sleeveless blouse. But I messed up on the shoes. I had never marched in a parade before, so I didn't realize my new white heels would kill me. The route was a mile long, and I could feel blisters first, then bleeding as the leather shoes pooled with sweat from the intense heat. I tried to keep smiling as I waved to the thousands of people, aware that all eyes were on Dad and me...but, oh, how my feet screamed in pain.

A man made me forget about the pain for a moment when he ran out from the crowd, got on one knee in front of me, and kissed my hand. He told a reporter he made it a point to try and kiss the hand of every elected official. "But Kara isn't an elected official," the reporter said.

"No, but she should be." Ha!

Dad beamed while reaching out for my hand and held it as we continued to march. No words were spoken, but I will always remember that this was first time he had held my hand for so long. Despite our sweaty palms, I didn't want to let go. He made me feel like Daddy's little girl.

It wasn't easy cramming a whole childhood into one summer, and as my father's and my experiences together wove golden threads in our tapestry, I wanted to make sure it was strong enough so it wouldn't unravel when I went off to college. We didn't have a lifetime of memories, but we were trying to make each day memorable.

My eighteenth birthday would be coming in two weeks, on July 16th, and I wondered if my father would think to make it special, like the 4th of July parade.

Mom had already started calling his secretary to make sure she put it on the calendar, so my father wouldn't forget.

"I wish I could be there with you, honey."

"I know, Mom, but we can celebrate when I get home." I felt the familiar grumble of guilt. I could tell she was sad to miss the big day, and it didn't seem fair she would not be the one to ring in my adulthood after all she'd done to get me there. Instead, she had just given my father the gift of a fully-grown daughter, and still hadn't gotten a thank you. I wondered what would happen with future holidays. Would I start to split up Christmas like some of my friends did with their divorced parents? This feeling of being split in half was something I'd never get used to.

But Mrs. Shuster, who had become so much more than a housekeeper to me, helped me over some of the rough patches. I had grown to love her because she seemed to understand that I was treading in unknown, scary waters, and had gone out of her way to make me feel welcome. But most importantly, she gave me a lot of insight into my father, to whom she was devoted.

She told me how my father never had a good relationship with his own father, and thought that was why he was so driven to succeed. Apparently, nothing ever seemed good enough for my grandfather, so every time my father won an election, succeeded in business, or achieved something great, it was like saying f%$# you, Walter, who was terribly hard on him as a kid. My father's younger brother, Wally, was seemingly Walter's favorite. Tragically, Wally died young of appendicitis, and my father was left to deal with his grief and wonder how he would measure up.

The grimace would splash across his face when talking about his disapproving, hard-driving father, and he kept it short by simply saying, "He was just not a nice man—but everyone loved my mother."

My father always spoke warmly about his mother, Jan, saying, "You couldn't find a single person who didn't genuinely like her."

Despite his resistance toward his father, there was no denying how much he looked like him. I could see the striking resemblance in pictures and assumed my father's tough shell was a product of my grandfather's making. Walter Sundlun was one of the first Jews to run for high office in Rhode Island. He lost his race for senate as a Republican, and I couldn't help but wonder if my father chose to be a Democrat just to be different from him.

Mrs. Schuster told me, "You are the best thing that ever happened to him. You make him so happy, and he smiles all the time now. He didn't use to do that. He may not know how to say it, but I can tell he really loves you."

I loved him, too, and her words were the best birthday present I could have asked for. But typical of her sweet nature, she'd insisted on giving me something to open. "It's not much, but I wanted you to have something from me on your birthday."

The gift bag was filled with all kinds of goodies that any girl could use: nail files, gum, hair ties, cuticle cream, and more.

"I love it!" I said, hugging her hard.

I'd been watching the clock all day. My father would be home soon, and I was glad for the balloon arrangement crowding the entryway. They'd serve as a tangible reminder for him about my birthday. I knew it had only been a month since we officially reunited, but things had been going so well, and I didn't want to have to hate him for doing something cold like forgetting the first birthday I would spend with him. Had the fates worked differently, this would have been the day I lost my rights to file suit against him. So much had happened, and I was glad he was now doing things without my having to force it. I wondered if he would get me a gift, or do something to show me his feelings were real.

We were supposed to go to a black tie event honoring the Navy that night, so I went upstairs to start getting ready so I wouldn't have to rush when he got home. A bit of panic rose up in my chest when I heard him enter the house. This was our first birthday together, and I didn't know what to expect.

I went downstairs in my bathrobe to say hello.

"Nice flowers," he said.

"Thanks, they're from my mom for my birthday. I'm officially an adult now," I said grinning.

"Happy Birthday! But you're still an infant in my book," he shot back with a grin.

"Thanks. I guess I'll go finish getting ready," I bit my lip as I scanned his hands and the table, as I passed by. It didn't appear that he had anything wrapped for me. Maybe it would come later?

He shouted upstairs to me, "It's black tie, you know."

"I know!" I shouted back downstairs. "I'm wearing a black dress."

"Perfect! We leave at 6:30. Sharp!"

My heart sank as I went back up to my room. Was he too busy to get a gift? Did it even register with him to get me a gift? *Come on, Kara, get over it. This whole summer is a gift!*

I came down into the kitchen with my hair slicked back and wearing a black cocktail dress.

"Va-va-va-voom," Mrs. Schuster said with a wide grin. "Don't you look special for your birthday!"

"Thanks, I feel special, too!"

My father came down looking handsome in his tux and bow tie. He was definitely not the clip-on kind of guy.

"That's a nice costume," Dad said while looking me over.

I stifled the urge to laugh. I quickly learned that he never referred to women's outfits as anything but costumes. This wasn't Halloween, and I definitely wasn't going trick or treating! "Thanks," I said, giving him a small curtsey. "I'm ready to go....and on time!"

After the trooper dropped us off at the event, we were escorted to the head table. When everyone finished their cocktails and dinner, my father got up to give his speech. It was hard to focus on what he was saying, since I was secretly pouting about my birthday and his lackluster acknowledgement thus far. He finished his remarks and sat down at the table next to me just as the Navy band came out tooting their horns and marching. After a few moments, I realized the tune was "Happy Birthday," and another group of navy men dressed in white were heading toward me with a cake covered in sparklers.

"Happy birthday, dear Kara, happy birthday to you," they sang as they set the cake in front of me. My father beamed, so proud that he had pulled off something special.

I didn't know what to say; my soldier father had just commanded the Navy to sing to me. I hadn't realized I was holding my breath, and now I could exhale, knowing he hadn't forgotten.

I blew out the candles and thanked my father, speaking as loudly as I could over the clapping throughout the room, before giving him a kiss on his forehead. I wanted everyone to see this was real. He kissed me back on my cheek, and I knew it would be a birthday I'd never forget. No, he didn't buy me an expensive gift, but it meant far more to me that he showed the world he cared. That was far more valuable, and exactly the display of affection I needed to feel like the dream wouldn't end when I left to go home.

~~

I was feeling more comfortable with my father, but I still had a lot to learn about the world he lived in. His was a world where turning eighteen meant having a debutante ball and "coming out" to Newport society. Meryl Page was my introduction to high society. Meryl and her brother, Blakely, lived in Hopedene, the mansion next door. She was a sweet, thin blonde who came across the lawn to introduce herself. "Welcome to the neighborhood. How are you liking everything?"

My mind raced with everything I'd seen and done so far. "I love it," I gushed. "What's not to like? Newport is amazing."

Meryl kindly offered to introduce me to her friends in town and invited me to go to what she called her "graduation party," but I later found out from my father it was her debutante ball, and there would be a big bash at Hopedene, the official name of the mansion next door. Of course, I accepted, but felt unprepared since I had no idea what to expect. For days I worried about what kind of gift I should get my new friend, how much should I spend, and who would pay for it? I didn't feel comfortable asking my father for money, and I don't think he thought about asking me if I had a dress or needed anything for the party. I decided to walk down to the small department store, Cherry and Webb, to look for gifts and see if there was something I could just buy on my own.

I scanned the glass cases for something that would jump out at me and say appropriate. I couldn't buy her clothes, make-up seemed wrong, and jewelry was too expensive. I decided on an adorable classic teddy bear that she could take with her to college. I wanted to show Meryl how grateful I was for her kindness by giving her something loving in return. I had it wrapped up, and wrote a nice card, wishing her well and thanking her for being my first friend in Newport.

The night of the party, my father and I walked over to Hopedene together, since he was invited as well. We walked hand-in-hand into the grand marble foyer, and I placed my gift next to some others that were left on a beautiful table. The numerous envelopes probably had money in them, and I worried I'd made a mistake, but it was too late to worry about it. I considered taking my gift back and bringing something later, but decided to just leave it. I wanted to ask my father about all of these things, but I felt embarrassed because I didn't already know. There were so many unwritten rules in my new world, and my best defense was to watch what everyone else did.

Walking past the water fountain and onto the terrace that overlooked a beautiful black-bottomed pool, with the Cliff Walk off in the distance, I felt like I'd stepped onto the set of *The Great Gatsby*. I tried my best to mask it, but I felt like I'd just been dropped into a secret society without the right password. I held my head up, watched my father, and tried to blend in while fervently wishing my new life had come with instructions.

My father put his arm around me and smiled at Meryl's mother and stepfather. "Chic, Britty, this is my daughter, Kara."

"You have such a beautiful home," I said while thinking how strange it felt to hear him use the word *daughter*. But I loved it, and looked forward to getting used to hearing it.

After a while, everyone was directed indoors to the formal room where the staircase emptied. I looked up and saw Meryl cascading down the stairs in a beautiful white gown—she looked like a real-life princess. The music played and people clapped, murmuring about how wonderful she looked and what a fabulous party this was. I remembered how she had called it a "graduation party." Bless her heart, I imagine she may have avoided calling it a debutante ball in order to make me feel more comfortable.

Even though this was Meryl's big night, I felt many eyes on me as my father led me around the party, introducing me to the people who made up Newport's social register. In a way, it felt like a coming out party for me, too. Every time he said "my daughter" he was validating my lineage in a place where bloodlines were everything. He could have kept me hidden, but instead, he was showing me off, and I knew he was proud of me. It dawned on me that I no longer needed a fairy godmother to go to the ball, and his invitation to be my father was not going to expire. But it all still felt like a dream.

Dayna would be the one to help me make it all feel real. My father told me I was welcome to invite a friend to come out and visit, and I was thrilled she agreed to come. I wanted someone from my old life to witness what was happening in my new world—someone to share all the excitement with and make it real. Dayna had been there to help me write my first letter to my father, and I needed her to be the bridge between my two lives.

I picked her up at the airport, and we giggled all the way back to my new house. I couldn't wait to show her all of my new favorite things, like walking on the Cliff Walk behind the famous mansions; eating lobster on Bannister's Wharf at the historic Clarke Cooke House restaurant; and basking in the sun at Bailey's Beach, the exclusive club my father belonged to, where we lazed on cushy lounge chairs in his oceanfront cabana sipping a mint freeze—a perfect blend of frozen lemonade with fresh mint.

"Wow, this is amazing," Dayna said as we pulled in to Seaward. "This is just so cool!"

"I know! Come on, I'll show you my room!"

We ran up the stairs to put her things away and freshen up before my father came home.

"So, he's kind of intimidating," I said, warning her, "but he's really a softy at heart, so just be yourself. Oh and...uh...don't chew gum around him—he hates it and says it's 'very un-lady like.' "

I wanted two of the most important people in my life to like each other as much as I loved them. What an odd feeling to know that my worlds were about to merge.

When he came home that night, he extended his hand to her. "Hi, Bruce Sundlun." —giving his standard greeting.

"Hi, I'm Dayna," she said, smiling sweetly.

"Wow, is everyone who grows up in Michigan short?" he said, laughing as he looked back and forth at us. It was hard for him to believe anyone was actually shorter than I was, but Dayna managed it.

"Very funny," I said sarcastically.

He looked at the shorts and t-shirts we were wearing, and made a suggestion: "Get dressed, you two, and I'll take you both out to dinner." After we ran upstairs and put on some dresses — our more appropriate "costumes" — my father took us to the Clambake Club, a private dinner club where Newport society dined on lobsters and other fresh seafood laid out on mirrors. Dayna stared at me, squeezing my hand, "Really, Kara?" she whispered, "*This* is your new life?"

The maître d' greeted us warmly. "Welcome, Governor."

"Thank you. I'd like you to meet my daughter and her friend from Michigan, Dayna Horton, who is visiting Newport for the first time. They'll both be attending the University of Michigan in the fall."

It felt utterly delicious to have Dayna witness him calling me his daughter out loud. I whispered to her that here in Newport, they always used first and last names with an introduction. To this day, Dayna and I still reflect on what an amazing summer we had together, and how much she fell in love with my father, how he loved her, too, nicknaming her Muscles, since she was so fit.

My father brought us both to work, and we would both take notes in the back of an economics conference preparing for the quiz he would give us later. She thought he was so fun to be around, and we could tell my father loved showing off two young girls to his friends. Dayna's visit allowed me to stop pinching myself because she was my witness that this magical summer wasn't a dream.

If having the time of my life vacationing with Dayna in a summer wonderland wasn't enough, I got offered my dream job at WPRI, then the ABC station in Providence. News Director Russ Kilgore wanted to give me a huge break to become an on-air youth reporter.

Now, I wasn't so naïve to think there wasn't a motive for their madness. My story had died down, and I was just getting used to life without a camera in my face, but the station thought putting me back on TV would be good for ratings. Their reasons didn't matter to me; I really wanted to work in television and this was my big shot. They had called Henry and asked him to broker a deal, but he said I would have to ask my father. I worried he'd say no. We had signed a gag order agreeing to stay out of the press unless it was something we both agreed to, and I couldn't see how this would benefit him. His advisors would no doubt think this was just going to shine the light back on the scandal they wanted to go away.

I knew I had to get up the guts to ask because, even at a young age, I was driven to establish my broadcasting career, and an on-air job—with pay, no less!—for someone with no experience was unheard of. As I dialed the State House, I crossed my fingers my father would let me do it.

"Okay, don't say no right away because I really, really want this." I took a deep breath and plunged in. "Channel 12 wants me to be an on air reporter. Can I do it, please, please, please?

Long pause.

"Kara, I don't know about this. Let me make some calls, and I'll get back to you."

Uh-oh. I began crossing everything on my body.

I would later learn my father called up the NBC station Channel 10, the one he used to run, hoping they would make me an offer, instead. He felt safer having me work there since, at the time, Channel 12 tended to lean toward the sensational. However, the more conservative station was not interested, so now my father had to make a tough decision.

Would he say no to protect himself and keep me out of the spotlight, or help me take a big step in my dream of becoming a reporter? I'm so happy he thought like a father instead of a Governor, and let me do it.

Henry negotiated the deal—they would pay me $1,000 for a three-part series and agree not to refer to me as the Governor's daughter. I would be announced only as their youth reporter, Kara Hewes.

Woo hoo! I couldn't wait to get to work!

I hugged my father when he came home, jumping up and down. "Thank you so much! I'm so excited!"

"Just remember to work hard. People will be watching everything you do because you're my daughter."

He was right, I could feel the eyes on me in the newsroom. The newspaper reported it wasn't fair that I got a job in such a competitive industry with no experience.

I'll be forever grateful to the awesome producer Nancy Dederian, and photographer Les Breault. They knew I didn't have a clue what I was doing, and helped me through every step. We decided I would report on anorexia and bulimia and how it was affecting teens in the area. I started making calls and lining up interviews, impressing Nancy with my hard work. She was happy we were getting such emotional interviews, since the girls felt safe opening up to someone their age. I felt bad working while Dayna was visiting, but one day Nancy told me to bring her with us. We were interviewing random people on the beach about eating disorders, and decided to use her in our story.

I asked her, "Do you think being thin makes someone attractive?"

"Honestly, I hate to admit it, but I really do think being thin makes someone attractive," Dayna answered looking skinny in her bikini and jean shorts.

I loved having my best friend on TV with me, and it was a great end to our time together. Dayna would have to go home, but I felt good knowing when I joined her at college she'd be the one friend who could understand everything that had happened to me over the summer.

Everything was perfect until the day before my series was set to air. I was running late, as usual, and I got stopped for speeding on the way to the TV station. I was driving my father's white campaign minivan with the license plate WIN 92. I had to pass through a section of Massachusetts that was famous for speed traps and very, very expensive tickets. If only I'd known.

The trooper looked down at me with my big purple Velcro rollers in my hair. "License and registration, please."

"I was on my way to work, sorry if I was going too fast."

"I clocked you at eighty-two miles an hour."

I winced. Eighty-two? Yikes! "Sorry," I mumbled. "Here's all my information."

"Sit tight."

I sat there sweating in my seat, wondering how big the fine would be. He came back about ten minutes later and handed me a ticket.

"Here ya go, everything you need is on this."

He never mentioned anything about my father, and neither did I, though I assumed he knew exactly who I was since my name was on my license and the van was registered to Governor Bruce Sundlun. How embarrassing! As I drove into the station, I knew I'd keep this as quiet as possible. However, by the time I got to work a totally different story was percolating.

Nancy pulled me aside. "The other stations are reporting you got a speeding ticket and tried to get out of it by saying 'Don't you know who I am?' "

I was dumbfounded. How could they report something so blatantly false? "Nancy, I swear it's not true. I didn't have to say anything, since I was in the campaign van that's registered to my father. They knew exactly who I was."

Nancy believed in me, but the question was whether the station would have to run the story as well, since it was making news.

"You need to call the reporters who are looking for you," Nancy said, "and I'll talk to management to see what they want to do."

The chill in the newsroom was palpable.

I had already been given a once-in-a-lifetime opportunity to go on the air as a teenager just because of who I was, and now it looked like I was a spoiled brat trying to get my Governor father to fix something else for me. I decided to just keep my nose down and do my work. But first, I had to call my father—a call I was dreading. My fingers shook as I dialed his office,

"Hello, Governor's office. May I help you?"

"Hi, it's Kara, may I speak to my father, please?" I hoped my voice wasn't quaking.

"One moment."

"Kara," he said sounding unhappy. *Oh God, he knows!* "What's this about you getting a speeding ticket and telling the police I'd take care of it for you?"

"Dad, I swear I didn't say that. I didn't say anything! All he did was write me the ticket."

"How much?" he asked.

"Um, I don't know, let me look…oh my God, it's $225."

"Well, you're going to pay every cent of that right away on your own. I don't pay traffic tickets."

"Of course—I'm so, so sorry—but I swear I didn't try to use your name." I had a sudden flash of fear that he'd tell me to go home.

Our relationship was just forming, and I needed him to know this was not who I was. I fought back tears, worried about the damage I might have done.

His voice softened a bit. "That's fine, Kara, just take care of this right away, okay? Goodbye."

It's easy to see now that my father was just trying to be a good parent by setting limits. But his disapproval made me sick with fear that I might lose all I'd worked for. Today I know those fears were unfounded and they were just leftover scars from the old wounds he'd created, but at the time, I was beyond scared. This was the first time he'd had to show me fatherly tough love in a way that would teach me a lesson. This was new territory, so every misstep got blown out of proportion in my mind.

Back in the newsroom, I was just hoping I didn't do too much damage to my job.

"Good news," Nancy said, putting her hand on my shoulder, "they aren't going to run the speeding ticket story, and your series will go on as scheduled." I exhaled for the first time in what felt like several minutes. "Thank you, Nancy. You have no idea how relieved I am."

The other stations ran with the false story, and I had no recourse other than to grit my teeth and bear it. But thankfully, the news cycle was short and my embarrassing moment was over quickly.

The next night we ran Part One of my taped series, and it went so well the news director came into the studio and asked me if I wanted to join the anchors live on the set for Part Two the next night.

At first, I felt like doing a handspring over stacked cars, but then the idea of LIVE TV — which meant sitting next to the avuncular Walter Cryan, who was the Cronkite of Rhode Island — made my knees shake. "Thanks so much," I said, hoping I sounded calm, "that sounds terrific."

Thankfully, my father had passed on his genes that allowed me to survive under pressure. Then again, just being his daughter gave me more confidence and determination to enter the industry where he'd been a Titan.

I really wanted my father to approve of the job I'd done, and couldn't wait to see him when he came home. We settled in for our usual Oreo cookies and milk in the study as I sat on pins and needles waiting for his opinion.

"You did great, young lady," he said with a proud smile, "and the folks at the station tell me you have been working really hard. Keep up the good work."

I could have danced on the ceiling! He approved! He thought I'd done a great job! "I hope you like the next two nights."

It was too soon to call him Dad, but my father was well on his way to becoming a real father. He had gone from presenting me as his new baby on the beach, to guiding me through my teenage misstep with the ticket, and now helping me into adulthood with my career as we neared the end of our time together. We had crammed a lot of growing into one summer, but I felt good knowing he wanted to do more to help me as I went off to college. I felt confident that our relationship would remain rock solid after I left in a few weeks.

~ *Photos* ~

People Magazine Article 1993   **First press conference in MI**

Answering questions with Henry Baskin

Reporters pack the State House for our first joint press conference

Dad and I having fun fielding questions

Cracking up at our first joint press conference at RI State House

Walking into State House for first joint press conference

Fenton and I at Narragansett Town Beach 1993

**Dayna and I: Clinton
Inauguration Party**

**My brothers and I
at Thanksgiving**

My first Thanksgiving - Salamander Farm 1993

Dad, Mom and me at Thanksgiving

Doing Dad's hair for a laugh

Black tie gala

My Internship at WPRI

**Fenton, Stuart, Mom, me, and Dad, at my college graduation
(Scholarship award)**

**President Clinton, me, RI Senator Claiborne Pell (Pell Grant)
and his granddaughter Tripler Pell**

Walking me down the aisle

Mom, Soozie and Marjorie kissing Dad at our wedding

Our wedding at Rosecliff 2003

Birth of Helena 2007

Bailey's Beach clambake with Helena

Helena playing with Poppy

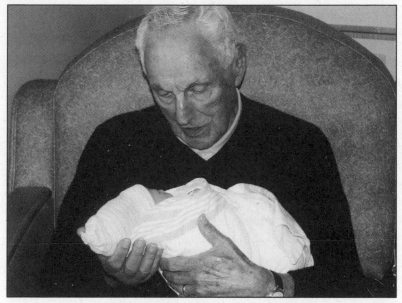

Dad holding newborn Julian 2009

Dad gives Julian a bottle

12 My Three Brothers

My father and I were having a great time getting to know each other, and I was feeling comfortable in the house. But until I met my brothers, the picture still felt incomplete. They were the final exam, and I knew their grades mattered. We were living in the honeymoon phase of a new relationship, where no one else is there to weigh in with their opinions. Though Marjorie and her son, Mark, had accepted me, my brothers and I shared the same blood, and I knew they meant a lot to my father. They had weathered four marriages, and I could only imagine how they felt about having a sister they'd never known about. I had always wanted a brother or sister, but these were grown men, old enough to be my father, and I was nervous about meeting them. What if they didn't like me? What if they thought I only wanted his money? What had my father told them about me?

My summer was winding down, and my father decided to have each brother come out to Newport to meet me before I left for college. So far, they'd only seen me on TV and read about me in the papers. It was time to make it real.

"We're working on getting the boys out here to meet you," my father said, making it more of an announcement—something he tended to do during awkward moments. "Tracy, my oldest, will come first, so make sure you're available this weekend,"

Finally! It's about time, Dad..."That's great! I'm excited to meet them."

When Tracy walked through the front door at Seaward, I couldn't believe how much he looked like my father. He had the same mannerisms and deep voice, but a lighter, goofier demeanor. While my father wore custom-made suits, Tracy, at forty-one, favored jeans, a bright colored shirt, and running shoes. He was in the business of putting on all the big track meets in New York City. His warm smile and sense of humor settled my nerves and put me immediately at ease.

"Hi...sis," he said, giving me a hug.

Phew, he's nice.

I hugged him back, smiling, "It's so nice to meet you, Tracy."

"You made this beautiful girl?" he asked, giving my father a salty grin. I could tell Tracy loved putting my father on the spot and making him squirm.

"Ha ha, very funny, Tracy, now get changed. I hope you're not wearing that garish shirt to dinner...and stand up straight!"

They were giving each other verbal noogies, but the love between them was apparent. How could I be nervous around all this?

My father arranged for us to have dinner at one of his favorite restaurants, The Clarke Cooke House, down on the wharf. We dined upstairs in the beautiful Skybar, where waiters wear white jackets and the social elite come for dancing. The maître d' stands at the top of the stairs to make sure no one enters who is not part of the "proper crowd." My father wasn't much for fancy food, but he liked to go where everyone knew his name, and this was just that sort of place.

At dinner, Tracy told the story of how he found out about me. "I was in a staff meeting, and my assistant told me Dad was on the phone. I told her to tell him I'd call him back. No, no, she says, it's urgent, so I took the call. Dad, I tell him, I'm in a meeting, what's so important that I can't call you back? He tells me that he's getting ready to have a press conference in fifteen minutes, and that it looks like I have a sister. After a brief pause, I say something sarcastic like

I guess the good news is it's not another brother. After he gives me the Cliff's Notes version of what happened, he asks if I'm upset. Yes, as a matter of fact, I am, I say. Really? he asks, sounding like his heart is sinking , and I say, well, yeah, Dad, I'm here in New York City and there's no way I can get to Providence in fifteen minutes! I'm going to miss one helluva press conference!"

We all laughed over our lobsters, and I knew I was going to like this man who, at twenty-three years my senior and old enough to be my father, was clearly opening his heart to become my brother.

He joked that considering Dad had been married four times and always loved women, he wasn't that surprised about me. "We always knew there could be more out there, so if you want to join this crazy family, all I have to say is welcome."

"Well, thank you," I said, laughing, "I'm happy to be here."

He had learned to love my father in spite of his flaws, just like I was trying to do.

Tracy shared Dad's drive for success and was the youngest Olympic track coach in history, having spent his career coaching elite athletes all over the world. At that time, he was in charge of the Metropolitan Athletics Congress in New York City, the regional arm of the national and international sports governing bodies for track and field. Today, millions of people run the Rock n' Roll Marathons he co-founded.

As I learned about what Tracy did, I couldn't help but share a knee slapper of my own. "You know my mother always told me I had a brother who was an Olympic swim coach, and that's why I joined the swim team. Guess we had the wrong sport!"

"Really? That's pretty funny. Well, can you run?"

I shook my head. "Nope, not at all, I hated track in gym."

I guess the star athlete gene skipped me. For our first few Christmases together, Tracy would send me running shoes, saying, "If you can run a mile, I can train you to run a marathon." I always told him that, unfortunately, I lack the most basic need for a marathon—desire. If I go to a race, he has me hold the finish line tape, since I'm better at smiling than running. Tracy and I bonded instantly that night, and I knew we were going to be able to build a real relationship because we both wanted to. Today, he is the best big brother I could hope for, and I always know I can count on him for advice or help if I need it.

After we came home from dinner, my father stifled a yawn. "Okay, you two, I'm beat and am going to bed. You kids have fun, and I'll see you tomorrow."

Our "good nights" trailed him up the stairs, knowing it was safe to have a more private conversation.

As an only child, I had missed out on late night conversations with a sibling, and I was looking forward to learning more about Tracy and my father. I knew Tracy could really fill in the blanks. I figured he had a lot of questions for me as well.

I grabbed some Oreos, and we settled in on the couch for our heart to heart. Our time was short, and we wanted to cover as much ground as we could, since there were eighteen years to catch up on.

"Listen, I'm happy to have you," Tracy said while stuffing an Oreo into his mouth. "I always wanted a sister, and this will be fun. I only wish Dad would have handled it better. I mean, we were all in Jamaica together for vacation after the DNA tests, and he didn't say a word. But that's Dad—he's not always the best with communicating."

"I know, it took me a while to get him to listen to me," I said honestly, "But I'm just so happy we're getting the chance to know each other now. I could have used a big brother growing up."

"I guess I heard the rumors about you, but I never did anything, and now I wish I had. We could have watched you grow up."

His acceptance was everything I'd wished for. Blood makes you related, but you can only become a family if the desire is there. Gratefully, it was.

Tracy rifled through his wallet and pulled out a picture of his baby girl, Felicity, my niece, and his wife, Isabel. I couldn't believe how much Felicity looked like my baby pictures. She had the same blonde hair with a curl at the ends and blue eyes. "Oh my gosh, Tracy, if you put my baby picture next to hers you'd think we were the same person." *Wow, I guess the blonde hair and light eyes comes from this side. I can't believe I have a twin.*

He looked at the photo with a gentle smile. "She's a beauty, I can't wait for you to meet her and Isabel."

"I look forward to that. I love babies."

As I look back through the years, watching Fifi grow up has been one of my greatest gifts. From the day when I bounced her on my knee at our first Thanksgiving together, we created a special bond. Not only does she look a lot like me—all grown up, working in the fashion industry after graduating magna cum laude from the University of Southern California—but she reminds me so much of myself, a determined only child who is ready to set the world on fire. She has that Sundlun dominance, but she also has her soft side when she cuddles my kids at the beach, which makes my heart melt. I'm so happy she's one family member I've gotten to know for almost her entire life.

That night, Tracy and I talked ourselves into the wee hours, until we finally forced ourselves to go to sleep so we could save ourselves for the next day. There was still so much to talk about, so I was grateful we would have a day of relaxing at the beach.

While eating breakfast the next morning, I watched my father came into the kitchen fully dressed in suit and tie, and raring to go. "Good morning," he said while reaching for a doughnut, "did you have a nice time last night?"

"We did. It was a late night, and I think Tracy is still asleep."

"You know, I've learned nothing good comes from staying up past midnight," he answered with a grin. Feeling groggy myself, I figured he was right on the money.

This Sunday wouldn't be a day of rest for my father. Sundays usually meant parades, potlucks, and other political appearances. Normally, he would have expected me to go with him and "learn something," but I got a reprieve with Tracy in town.

"Listen, why don't you take the day and spend some time with Tracy. I'll call you when I'm done."

"That's a great idea, thanks. Don't work too hard," I said, waving to him and the trooper as they left for what I assumed would be a long day.

I was excited for a beach day. If my father had been with us, it would have meant spending the day at Bailey's Beach club, which was certainly not a punishment. But since we were on our own, Tracy and I decided to go to the public beach in Narragansett, where the waves were bigger and we could meet cousin Fenton, who refused to step foot in the private beach club.

It was the perfect day for relaxing and baking in the sun, and I was excited to get to have some great bonding time with the new family. We walked the sandy shores, drank the famous frozen Del's lemonade that you'll only find in Rhode Island, and laughed so much my face hurt.

Fenton was thrilled to share his story about the press conference to Tracy. "You should have been there. It was amazing—she's a star, and so much like your father."

"I can see that. She's just lucky she's a girl, since Dad was always better with women." He shot out a good-natured laugh. Had my father been harder on his sons than he was being with me?

Fenton stood up and grabbed my arm. "C'mon, let's take a walk. Some kids I know are dying to meet you, and I promised I'd introduce them to 'Kara from TV.' "

While I was shaking hands and talking to some of the kids, I heard something that sounded like my name over the loudspeaker. I turned. "Hang on…Fenton, did you hear that?"

"What?"

Then I heard it again: "Kara Hewes, please come to the front desk, Kara Hewes, please report to the front desk."

Fenton smacked his forehead. "Oh my gosh, your father must be looking for you. He's the only one who could be paging you at a public beach."

Long before everyone had a smartphone my father knew how to find someone anywhere. I had to run across the hot sand to the check-in desk, "Hi, I'm Kara Hewes," I said in between catching my breath.

The lady handed me the phone. "Governor Sundlun is on the line for you."

Uh oh..."Hello?"

"Kara, this is your father. I've been home for almost an hour now. I've called everywhere looking for you!" I could hear the anger in his voice. Oops.

"Uh, we came to Narragansett beach to see Fenton. I thought you wouldn't be home until much later."

"No, I'm home now, and I was going to take you both out for a late lunch, but I guess I'll have to eat alone." Hmm, was he pouting?

"No, no, don't do that. Let me grab Tracy, and we'll be home right away."

His reply was short and curt. "Goodbye."

Now, most teenagers would have found their father paging them at a beach more than a little intrusive, but it felt good that he was worried about me. Sure, he was acting like a baby, but it proved to me he really wanted to hang out with Tracy and me. As promised, we raced home. My father was used to beckoning people, and this was no exception. Under normal circumstances, I would have been ticked off, but my life was anything but normal, and I liked being summoned because it made me feel important to him.

Back at home, we found my father sitting in the kitchen in his bathrobe, eating a donut. Yep, he was definitely pouting. His always-perfectly-coiffed hair was disheveled, and I couldn't help but smile because I'd never seen him like this.

"I've been home all alone, waiting for you two and had no idea where you were! I wanted to take you to Bailey's for lunch—not even a note!"

"Dad, you said you wouldn't be around, so we did our own thing," Tracy countered, with much more confidence than I had.

"Dumb, dumb! You are both dumb, dumb!" he said, sounding more like a hurt four-year-old than a tough governor.

My father was having a good old-fashioned meltdown because he missed us, and I'm sure it surprised him as much as it did us. His was such a simple, organic reaction, that my heart melted. He'd wanted to be with us and, rather than simply saying that, he hid his feelings by rebuking us. Thing is, he didn't fool anyone.

So what do you do when you have someone trying to act like he's rough and tough, but showing he's really a softie? You test the limits and inject some humor. "Oh, poor baby," I cooed, walking over to where he was sitting. "We are so sorry!" I pulled out a brush from my beach bag. "Here, let me fix your hair...it's a mess."

My father shot me stern look, but didn't stop me from brushing his thick lion-like white hair.

"What on earth are you doing?" he said, trying to sound gruff.

"You'll see…"

I pulled his hair into a bunch and used the elastic on my wrist to tie it into a ponytail on top of his head à la Pebbles from *The Flintstones*.

Tracy and Mrs. Schuster doubled over laughing, while my father sat crunching his brows together and refusing to unwrap his arms from across his chest. I pulled out my camera and started to take ridiculous pictures of him with his bathrobe and pony tail on top of his head.

Tracy just shook his head. "See? I told you a girl can get away with a lot more with him."

So many times, we had fallen on humor to escape awkwardness, and I could tell by the softening in my father's brow that this was starting to work. Try as he might, my father's stern gaze melted into laughter.

"Okay, okay, now get this out of my hair, and let's get dressed…and no more running off anymore without telling me where you are!"

Whatever ice was there between me and my new family was being broken. Humor really was the best elixir.

The weekend went by too fast, and Tracy and I promised to stay in touch. "Once you get up to school, I'll call you on Sundays." And he'd kept his promise, often checking in from various cities around the world — in spite of his demanding schedule. Like my father, work made Tracy tick. He was a master at his profession, and he couldn't separate it from who he was. Every time he took time out of his busy life to call me, I knew it was his way of trying to make things right, and I loved him for it.

My youngest brother, Peter, was the next to visit. He was coming from Richmond, Virginia, and I hoped we would have as much fun as I'd had with Tracy. I felt more confident knowing at least one brother approved of me. When Peter walked through the door, it was like déjà vu. He was a taller blond version of my father and Tracy. "Hello, hello!" he said, giving me a big welcoming hug. "It's so nice to meet the new family member in person." He was alluding to having heard the rumors about me over the years and seeing the newspaper articles.

I smiled. "It's great to meet you too — for real."

Then he looked at our father shaking his head, "You needed a paternity test? Look in the mirror!"

Wow, now *that's* an ice breaker. We both laughed as our father shrugged his shoulders — uncharacteristically speechless.

Peter talked about when my father told him about me and the news conference. He took it in stride like Tracy. "I told him he lost an engine, feather it."

Peter had followed my father's love of aviation by becoming an airline pilot. But that's where the similarities ended. Peter showed a sensitive, perceptive side that wasn't as apparent in my father or Tracy. Where my father was tough and brief, Peter told long, loving stories about his wife, Karen, and I knew he was a good man who believed in the importance of family. He was also the only one who had ever met my mother.

"I'm sorry I didn't come and see you when you were a baby. Your mother called me, you know."

I was touched that he was trying to make amends, but I could hardly blame him for anything. "I know, she told me. But it's okay. I know there was probably nothing you could have done."

He shook his head. "No I should have. I was just a college kid when your mom called and asked me to come meet my sister. I called Dad and he told me to stay out of it, so I did. I wish so much now I had done something different, and we all could have known you."

As great as all this made me feel, I could tell there was a "but" coming.

"But why did you have to make things so public? Why couldn't you just reach out to us in a private way?"

It was a valid question, and my heart went out to him. "I never wanted this to become a huge media circus. The problem was I did try to reach out privately. I wrote letters, and even after I met him and the DNA test proved I was his daughter, he still refused to acknowledge me. I felt like I had no choice. I never wanted to hurt anyone."

He nodded slowly. "Well, that makes sense. It sounds like him," he said with an "I know it all too well" undertone. "You know, he wasn't around much for us either. He's a businessman first and family man somewhere down the list." I could tell he still carried the hurt.

The one thing Peter did inherit from my father was an analytical mind. After our weekend together he seemed satisfied that I had answered all of his questions, and he was ready to embrace me just like Tracy had. Today, Peter is the one brother I can count on to never miss anyone's birthday, and always calls on holidays. He is a wonderful father to his son, Hunter, and devoted husband to Karen for more than twenty-five years now. And he's the only one in our family who is handy, often fixing all the little broken things in my house when he comes to visit. He chose to live life differently than my father, and though he is a pilot, he's anything but a jetsetter, preferring to be home to go to all of Hunter's swim meets and help with homework. I often think he healed himself through the love he gives to his family, and I am happy to be on the receiving end of his sincerity.

The last to visit was my middle brother, Stuart, the handsome bachelor with the thick curly hair and blue eyes that apparently came from his mother. He was a jetsetter like Dad, doing business all over the world, but also sweet and funny, like the boy next door.

He was wearing his trademark blue Lacoste shirt and Levis when he arrived at Seaward after taking a train from New York City, where he lived on the Upper East Side.

"Hello! So nice to meet you," he said hugging me right away.

"I'm so happy you're here, I have heard a lot about you."

From everything I'd heard, Stuart was the special one. Like my father, he went to Harvard, and was a great athlete, and was now making his mark in the world of finance.

Over dinner, Stuart told me how he'd first heard about me, which was a carbon copy of how Peter and Tracy had found out, only by the time my dad called Stuart he was running out of time, and even more brief. "Dad called me up and says, it's your father, I'm having a press conference in fifteen minutes, you have a sister, I've gotta go. By the time I stammered out an 'okay,' he'd hung up. Click! That was it."

You would think these stories made my father cringe, but he didn't say anything—as if he embraced his perfect imperfections. Instead, we all just laughed, since that was *so* my father. His abruptness was part of what made him who he was, and my brothers had learned to expect it. I was learning my new family was unabashedly honest, despite its deficiencies, and I think that's why my brothers took to me so easily. They had learned to roll with the punches. After four marriages, and several step kids, nothing seemed to surprise them anymore. My father was who he was, and you could drive yourself nuts, or just focus on the good—and laugh at the rest.

I looked forward to getting Stuart's story of how he really felt about my arrival when we could be alone. In the meantime, my father seemed happy that all of his sons were being so open to me, especially since he had clearly kept a lot from them in the past few years.

When we got back home, Stuart and my father took off their blazers and ties, and we all sunk into the couch in the study for the traditional Oreos and goodnights. Just like with Tracy and Peter, Stuart and I stayed up in the study talking about life.

"Well, are you okay with all that's happened?" I asked in between bites of Oreos. "What do think about all of this—about me?"

"I feel great, Kara. You're smart, you're pretty, what else is there to worry about?"

It was obvious Stuart had inherited my father's suave manner, and it was clear they both had the ability to make women love them. I had heard Stuart was living with the famous model Margaux Hemmingway since they were both in a *People Magazine* story together, and he was featured in her *E! True Hollywood Story* as the businessman who helped her recover from alcoholism.

"Well, I guess we both have *People Magazine* in common," I said, trying to crack a joke.

"That's true," he beamed back.

Stuart was brilliant and could talk about anything, but he spoke *to* me, not *at* me. He was the easy-to-get-along-with middle child, and I felt proud to have a "cool" brother like him.

Stuart visited Newport often that summer, since he loved to spend weekends playing tennis and relaxing at Bailey's Beach, where he was also a member. He was gracious and kind by always introducing me to everyone as his "sister." When some people gave him a funny look and remarked about not knowing he had a sister, he would laugh and say, "Neither did I!"

Just like our father, he knew how to use humor to change the mood.

Sometimes my father tried to encourage Stuart to settle down. "You're wasting your life, you need to get married and have children."

Stuart would roll his eyes — it was obvious he'd heard this many times. "Someday, Dad, someday," he said, unfazed by my father's prodding. He knew how to placate his commander.

Stuart has a heart of gold, but I wonder if he avoided marriage in fear that he might be wired too much like our father, and didn't want to end up with the same bad track record. Today, he is a wonderful uncle to my two children. They call him "Uncle Jungle Gym," since they love to climb on his big strong shoulders. He spends nearly every weekend at our home in Newport during the summer, and I love watching him go from buying toys for the kids at a Thomas the Train outing, to a black tie gala where the ladies are waiting for a dance. He may never be the type to settle down, but I'm so happy when he presses the Pause button, it's with me.

As a journalist who covers spirituality on my talk show, I have met many gurus who speak about past lives and say we are part of a soul group that chooses to incarnate time and time again to learn our lessons on Earth. I'm not sure where I am with all that, but all I can say for sure is that my brothers didn't feel new to me. Just like it was with my father, the connections we shared were easy and strong. Filling in my family tree with smart, successful men made me feel more grounded. Their love settled in my core and made me feel more solid.

My brothers and I represent pieces of my father. He had been a runner like Tracy, a pilot like Peter, a businessman like Stuart, and a broadcaster like me. We are all spokes of the same wheel, connected at the center by our love for and likeness to this man who helped shape who we became.

As summer drew to a close, we promised to keep in touch and meet at my father's home in Middleburg, Virginia for Thanksgiving. My brothers were now the borders to my tapestry, with all four of us now joined in a way that assured me it wasn't going to unstitch the minute I turned my back and went off to college.

The day I left, I hugged my father goodbye at the same threshold where my new life had begun a few short weeks ago. He squeezed me extra hard. "Make sure you call when you get home to Michigan to let us know you made it okay."

"I will. And thank you for everything—I'll miss you so much."

"I'll be in touch," he said smiling, but I could see in his eyes that he'd miss me, too.

I hadn't called him Dad yet, but with a little more time, I knew I would. I just wanted it to be special.

I had to teach my father how to share his feelings, and that would take time. In later years, he never hung up without saying "I love you," but it took many times of me saying it first. It's not that he didn't care, he was just afraid to show it—or didn't know how. Eventually, we both felt safe enough to open our hearts—and it started with him opening his home that summer.

My father had a state trooper escort me to the airport. I gazed out at the ocean as we pulled away from Seaward, and a part of me wished I could stay forever. My life had been indelibly changed, and I didn't want the dream to end. This time, there were no cameras waiting for me at the airport. Finally, the show was over, and I was so grateful we had created something real.

13 A Whole New Me

August, 1993

I came back home to Mom's open arms. "I missed you so much," she said, squeezing me.

"I missed you, too." And I did. But looking at her and our apartment, nothing felt the same. I was looking at my life here through a new filter, and I felt like I'd just stepped back in time. I needed to find my footing. My entire being had been transformed in a life-altering way, while nothing back home had changed at all. I needed to readjust to the old world, all the while knowing that very soon, another new world would open at college. I was standing in limbo land.

More than anything, I didn't want to hurt my mom, so I didn't say much about private beach clubs and helicopters. Instead, we set off to do our favorite thing together—shopping! This time the trip would be a rite of passage as we set out to get everything I needed for my college dorm room. Mom had already secured a great deal on a green and white striped mini couch that rolled out to a bed, much more chic then a typical futon she thought, and it would still fit in my tiny dorm room below the loft bed my roommate and I were going to have built by the college guys on campus on move-in day.

Today was about Mom helping me buy the bedding, cute accessories, and plenty of plastic storage to set up my new abode in academia. As we strolled the aisles of the Bed Bath and Beyond on Orchard Lake Road in West Bloomfield, I could feel the eyes of other shoppers looking at Mom and me as we squeezed different pillows to see which would be most comfortable. Then came the whispers. In the midst of this very normal errand, I suddenly remembered that my life was anything but normal now. After spending an exhilarating summer with Dad in Newport, I was looking forward to some Joe Schmoe days back at home, and was quickly realizing there was no more normal.

"Hi, are you Kara Hewes?" The questions came from a mom who was shopping with her daughter.

I nodded. "Yes"

"I thought so, I just want to say I am so proud of what you and your mom did. So brave."

"Thanks," my mom said proudly. "I raised her to be a tough cookie."

"You did a great job," the woman answered.

Mom smiled, energized by the compliments, and I was happy she was getting the credit she deserved. But standing there in that store with strangers who came up to us, it hit me that the genie was out of the bottle and, like it or not, we were now famous, which meant people were going to be watching and judging us. The new level of distinction and the feeling that Mom could still crumble at any moment had me walking on eggshells. I was back in the world where I had to be the protector, and I sorely missed the safety I'd felt when my father ran the show and protected me.

The problem was, Mom felt anything but safe, thanks to my father. It had only been about two months since he called her a golddigger, and I knew she was still hurting. I had inherited a thicker skin from my father, but Mom's was paper thin, so she felt insults deeply, and it was hard for her to let go. While I had spent a summer healing my hurts with laughter and exciting moments, Mom stayed stuck on Pause. My father hadn't done anything to heal her, and I wished there was some magic to make her better. I really wanted our last couple weeks together to be peaceful before I moved off to school, so I tried to tread carefully and avoid talking too much about my father, or how amazing my summer in Newport had been.

When move-in day at the University of Michigan arrived, Mom helped me load up the car to drive to Ann Arbor for the big send off. We waited in long lines of traffic trying to get close to South Quad, the dorm I would move into on the 7th floor. My roommate, Ellie, was a friend from my high school, and we were so excited to discover that we'd gotten one of the coveted rooms with a sink—which meant we wouldn't have to go down the hall to the communal bathroom every time we wanted to brush our teeth or get water. However, Mom was less than excited about hauling all of my things up seven flights of stairs to our coveted room. This was a job for a strong man, of which we saw plenty in the form of fathers lugging duffle bags into the dorm. But, once again, Mom was doing the heavy lifting on her own. With each box we lugged, she got more ticked off.

"Kara this is just too much, I'm going to get some guys to help us."

"No, Mom, we can do it," I said, feeling annoyed we couldn't do this rite of passage alone, yet painfully aware of Ellie's father helping with the heavy lifting.

Mom insisted she didn't want to do the job and was going to get us help. "I'm not strong enough. I'm going to pay some college boys to finish." Then the elephant in the room reared its head. "If your father is so great, why isn't he here to help move you in?"

"Mom, come on, he's seventy-three years old. He can't be lugging all this. Besides, he has to be in Rhode Island to run the state."

"Why are you always defending him?" Mom shouted.

"Stop yelling, everyone is looking at us!" I yelled back, only calling more attention to us. "Why can't this just be a great day like it is for normal families?" I felt the heat of rage boil up inside of me. *Normal.* Normal was that elusive quality I was forever seeking.

Outraged, she came back at me. "Do you yell at your father like this? Why, you treat him so much better than your own mother, who raised you alone!"

There it was—all the hurt and ugliness unleashed itself from the well of fury and resentment that Mom had carried my whole life. How I wished she could snap out of it, but she just couldn't jump over the crater in her soul. She'd loved him, and he'd hurt her. She'd had his child and he had ignored us. Her reality was different than mine, and there was nothing I could do about it except bear the brunt of her frustration.

But Mom had a point. I was being a brat and wouldn't have acted like this to my father. I wouldn't have yelled at him or talked to him in a disrespectful tone because he was too new. My relationship with Mom was older, more tested, and filled with the comforts that allowed fighting and criticism, because we knew the long-standing love would allow us to bounce back like rubber.

Mom and I were durable, strengthened by the test of time. My father and I were more like the fragile fine china that's only brought out on special occasions, always careful not to scratch or chip the porcelain. My father's relationship had not been tested for everyday use yet—it hadn't been toughened up by typical teenage fights because I'd always used my best manners around him. Heck, I was still at the point where I avoided calling him anything since I didn't know how to refer to him. His first name sounded cold, and he hadn't earned the title of Dad yet.

None of this was fair to Mom—I knew that—but it was the way it had to be now. Even with my father in our lives, writing the checks for college, Mom would still be the one to do the dirty work of day to day parenting. My father wasn't the type to wear overalls, and I was too scared to ask him to help me move since it wasn't in our agreement.

After the guys finished hoisting my last box up the cold industrial stairs, Mom and I sank down into the tiny couch she bought me and called it a day.

"Thanks, Mom." I reached out and touched her arm. "I'm sorry we fought."

She gave me a weary smile. "I'm sorry, too. I'm so proud of you. You're going to do great here."

"Thanks. Love you."

"Love you, too," she said, hugging me.

I walked her downstairs and gave her a lingering hug before she got in her car. As I watched her drive away, I was struck that, for the first time since having me, she could finally focus on her own life. I was grown, and it was now my father's job to cover my education. The burden of being a single mother was finally being lifted, but with that, she was also losing her exclusivity. Now she was forced to share me with the man who'd never shared any responsibility for me. I wanted Mom to be just as happy, but she was starting her next chapter of life all alone, and I considered the same fear that had become a running theme; I'd gained a father and lost my mother.

My new identity was only three months old, and it felt like a borrowed sweater that didn't exactly fit me right. When I had to talk about myself to new friends, I was never sure what to say about my family or background. I had grown up as an only child of a single mother, and now all of a sudden I was a Governor's daughter with three older brothers. I was a Midwesterner, but if I said who my father was, one assumed I was from the East Coast. Rather than spending twenty minutes explaining my unique situation, it was easier not to say anything.

As I tried to find my way around campus, my father let me know he was still thinking of me with frequent phone calls to my dorm room, usually at 6 a.m., when he knew we were fast asleep.

"Kara, it's your father, just want to say good morning and make sure you're studying," he would say with a chuckle.

"No, actually we're all sleeping," I would answer in a groggy whisper.

"Oh, so sorry, have a good day." Click. Short and sweet — that was my father.

It was adorable that he wanted to say hi and let me know I was on his mind before his day began, but there's little doubt my roommate found this very annoying. This was also his way of letting me know he was already up and conquering the world. He used to call the Lieutenant Governor, Robert Weygand, and wake him up every morning when he crossed into a section of Massachusetts because, according to an archaic state law, he wasn't governor when he left the state.

"Hello, I'm just calling to say you're the governor, so wake up," he would say, laughing before hanging up. Ten miles later, he'd call back and tell Weygand he could go back to bed since he was the governor again.

Back at school, it was time for sorority rush, and though I didn't want to engage in the catty, mindless activities that were sometimes associated with being in a sorority, I did want to find a way to make the campus of thirty-five thousand people feel smaller, and build a new community of friends. But I would have to ask my father for the dues to join a sorority.

"Please, I think it will really help me with a great place to live and some wonderful connections."

"I don't know…are you sure that's a good idea?"

"I do! The Greek system is respected on this campus, I promise."

"Okay, but this better not turn into a big party that keeps you from studying."

"Thank you so much! And I promise I'll keep my grades up."

Brooke and Dayna planned on rushing, too, but we all had agreed to go our own ways in order to branch out and meet new friends. Our friendship was cemented in granite, and we would always have each other. They would always be the witnesses to me before I'd gained a father.

~

The first day of rush, I met Laura, a stunningly beautiful blonde girl from New Jersey who had curly hair like me. She was like a ball of light, and we sparked an instant friendship. Even though her blue-green eyes and curvy shape made the boys speechless, she was quick and bright. We discovered that we lived in the same dorm and ended up liking the same sorority, Kappa Alpha Theta. Not only was it the oldest sorority, founded by a young woman who thought girls should have fraternities, too, but we got to live in one the most beautiful old mansions in Ann Arbor, complete with antique furnishings, comfortable rooms, and a great meal plan.

Laura and I got in and immediately bonded. After teaching her how to straighten her curly hair, it got to the point where people started to confuse us.

As close as we were becoming, I hadn't shared my story with Laura as yet. She knew my father was the governor of Rhode Island—I just left out the part where I'd only met him three months earlier. I wasn't sure how to bring it up, so I kept waiting for the right time.

It was Heather, another new friend, who ended up helping me let the cat out of the bag. Laura had introduced me to Heather, who was from Philadelphia... and so tiny that she made me look like a giant. What she lacked in size, she made up for in her ability to make a big splash with her storytelling—which earned her the nickname Hollywood. Seemed like destiny that her ability to tell a big story would bump up against my tale that seemed made for the movies.

The three of us had become a tight threesome, and I wondered when and how I would share my whole story. As usual, Fate stepped in. Heather's grandfather called her up one day after reading the *People* magazine article and told her about the girl who sued the governor of Rhode Island and was going to the University of Michigan. Since it was such a big school, Heather naturally assumed she wouldn't know the girl from the article until Pop Pop read her the name—Kara Hewes.

"Holy cow, Pop Pop, she's one of my closest friends!" Heather exclaimed, telling Laura and me the story.

Phew, that took care of my problem about how to tell Laura. Now everyone knew, and I could finally relax, knowing the secret was out.

As my new friends learned my story, my identity started to feel more real, and I was relieved that their reactions were positive.

Another good friend, Lauren, who came from Cleveland, remembered watching my story on TV all summer long before leaving to college, and thought my life sounded like a novel, though there were times when I wondered if it didn't more closely resemble a soap opera.

My freshman year was going great. I was making new friends and happy to tell Mom and my father that I was doing well in my classes. I looked forward to sharing my stories about college life with my father and brothers at the Sundlun family Thanksgiving, though I felt guilty leaving Mom for the first time on a holiday. After promising I would drive home for a weekend soon, I packed my bags for what everyone called "the farm" in Middleburg, Virginia. To me, anything with the word "farm" in it meant jeans, Timberland boots, and warm sweaters, so I was alarmed to discover I had the wrong idea. This wasn't a place of cows and chickens, but rather a 170 acre estate for fox hunting. Instead of a humble ranch house with a creaky screen door, I walked into an elegant stone home, complete with a carriage house that was grander than Dad's Cliff Walk estate.

"Welcome to my farm," my father said taking my bags from me and giving me a hug hello. "I think you'll love it here."

"Wow," I said, looking at the shiny silver sitting on top the fine antiques, "it's beautiful...um...so much fancier than I expected."

"Oh, we do okay," he said with a small grin. "Mary Lou will help you get settled," my father said.

I liked Mary Lou, the housekeeper, right away—as much as Mrs. Schuster. "C'mon, I'll show you to your room and get you some soup I just made."

Now this was the way to come home for the holidays!

Mary Lou walked me down a long hallway filled with beautiful antiques and sliver, then up a long spiral staircase with shiny wooden spindles to my room. I couldn't believe this was my father's *second* home. When we arrived at my room, the crisp white linens reminded me of my old bed in the "Blue Room" back in Newport.

Wow, life with my father is just full of surprises. Very lovely and fun surprises!

When I came back downstairs, my father told me his plans. "I'm having a dinner party tonight, so why don't you rest up and be ready by seven p.m."

Panic rose up in my throat, since I knew I had the wrong clothes. "Okay, but I have to tell you that when you said farm, I thought Old McDonald, so I only brought jeans and sweaters." I hoped he wouldn't be mad.

He folded his arms and put on a thoughtful expression. "Hmm. Well, that's not going to work. Come with me—we're going to have to go to town and get you a dress."

We hopped in the car and sped off for our first father-daughter shopping trip. He squeezed his big white Jeep Grand Wagoneer with wooden side paneling into a street parking space, and led me into a beautiful boutique.

"Do you have any black dresses in small sizes?"

The sales lady quickly gathered up all she had and placed them in a fitting room, then escorted my father to a big comfy chair. Each time I tried on a dress, my father had me come out and model it for him, where he would quickly dismiss one he didn't like with the shake of his head or a crinkle of his nose. I'll say this for him; he had an eye for style, and wanted me to look a specific way to meet his foxhunting friends. I was worried about the price tags, since some of the dresses were several hundred dollars, but he never asked about the cost—he just wanted it to look good. Finally, we settled on a knee length black cocktail dress and a strand of large pearls to go with it.

As he handed the lady his credit card, he said, "Let me tell you a lesson about packing that I learned from Jackie Kennedy: A woman should never leave home without a black dress, a strand of pearls and a houndstooth suit. If you have all that you will be fine for any social occasion."

"Ok, I'll remember that next time," wondering where I would ever need a houndstooth suit at the age of eighteen.

That night, we sat with my father's friends in the formal dining room while Mary Lou served homemade borscht soup in china bowls. I'd always thought I hated beets, but I was hooked after tasting Mary Lou's.

During dinner, Marjorie made a toast welcoming me to the family, then said something that caught us all off guard: "I always told Bruce that when his daughter came looking for him, he should open his heart, and I would, too."

Marjorie's announcement clearly clashed with Dad's position that he didn't know I was his—but no one said anything.

The next day was Thanksgiving, and we had a glorious turkey dinner on more beautiful china. I enjoyed relaxing with my brothers and meeting my sisters-in-law, Karen and Isabel, for the first time. They were both gracious and sweet, and it felt great to have some females around.

Karen hugged me gently, saying how happy she was to meet me. Isabel was equally warm, but mindful of my baby niece, Felicity, crawling around her feet. Felicity was such a cute baby, I got down on the floor and bounced her on my stomach while everyone remarked over our strong resemblance. Cousin Fenton was there as well, and enjoyed telling everyone he was the first relative to meet me at the State House.

Our first holiday together as a family could have been so awkward, but instead I felt so at ease. It had been such a wild journey since the first family dinner for the cameras. Back then we *called* each other family, but now we were *becoming* a real family.

The Sundlun family Thanksgiving tradition continues to this day, only now that my father is gone, we celebrate at my house. The quarters are a bit more cramped than my father's lavish farm, but we love overflowing on couches for one weekend a year to celebrate our family. We put my father's picture out and repeat his favorite sayings, like "Lead, follow, or get out of the way," when we're trying to get everyone seated. I always serve my father's favorite drink, hot apple cider—and we go through gallons of it.

When we go around the table to give thanks, family is always first on our gratitude list. No one could have predicted twenty years ago that this story would end with dinner being served at my table. I am forever grateful I made the choice to follow that small voice deep inside that urged me to keep the faith—that my father would come around. If I hadn't, just think of we all that we would have missed. Because of my choice to have faith and forgive, my children have the kind of family I so badly wanted growing up.

Leaving the farm after my first Thanksgiving, we all promised to stay in touch with Sunday calls until we met again for a winter vacation at my father's home in Jamaica.

As promised, I spent a nice Christmas with Mom, then headed off to Montego Bay for a Sundlun family vacation at my father's villa in Round Hill, a fancy resort where Ralph Lauren and other celebrities were known to take their holidays. This was home number three, and just as spectacular as the rest—which, of course, left me breathless. He had bought the home after the government shut down travel to Cuba, where he used to take his holidays. Looking around the five bedroom villa that sat on a hill surrounded by tropical flowers, I decided my father had made a terrific decision.

The only thing he insisted upon is that we all have breakfast together before setting out to enjoy our days, which wasn't that tall an order since I eagerly bounced out of bed to get those yummy fried banana pancakes the staff made for us each morning.

During the day, I basked in the sun and enjoyed playing with Fifi in the ocean. At night we dined on jerk chicken and other island favorites while my father held court at the dinner table. It was fun to see him in a relaxed setting, because I got to see a different side of him. He traded in his double breasted suits and black ties for brightly colored pants and unbuttoned shirts. The change of clothes seemed to melt away the tough exterior, and I saw that he actually did know how to let his hair down. One night, we were having such a good time, and my father impulsively held out his hand to me. "You want to dance?"

"Well, of course," I said taking his hand, but feeling a bit nervous, since I'd never danced with him before. He twirled me around to the beat of the steel drum band and, once again, I felt the urge to pinch myself. How could life be this good?

I went back to school and noticed an interesting shift. A boy named Doug had shown up in my life. What felt strange was that he wasn't like the bad boys I had dated in high school. Doug was smart, grounded, and came from a good family. He was someone I could take home to meet my father, and I couldn't help but wonder if these deposits of fatherly love changed me to the point where I was now attracting a better kind of guy. I finally felt worthy of demanding more from the men in my life, and it appeared to be showing up in every area of my life. I know now that poor male relationships are a classic symptom in fatherless girls because we often subconsciously recreate the feeling of abandonment, since that is all we have ever known. The entry of my father into my life, even though I was an adult, wasn't too late to have a profound effect on my future relationships. It's the very reason why I believe it's never too late to heal.

As my freshman year came to a close we were approaching what would be our first real Father's Day together. The year before I'd known my father less than a week, and had given him a basic card. This time it meant something. A lot, in fact. So I wanted to get him something special, something that would show him I knew he was trying hard. In the past year of getting to know my father, I had avoided calling him anything, since it didn't feel right to call him Dad yet.

One of the state troopers, Al Pontarelli, kept teasing me. "When are you going to start calling him Dad?"

"In time. He has to earn it."

The truth was, I thought my father had proven himself throughout this transformational year of firsts, and I wanted to call him Dad, but I couldn't make the word come out yet. It felt like it should be a special occasion, so I decided get him something to mark the significant transition

After a trip to the mall, I settled upon a mahogany memory box. I knew my father loved to save things, and I thought it would be a perfect safety deposit box for our future mementos. I went to the Things Remembered store to engrave a golden metal plaque with the name DAD in all capital letters and the date June 20, 1994 under it. I was moving back to Rhode Island for the summer again and decided I would give it to him on Father's Day in person. When I handed him the heavy gift to open, he ripped the wrapping paper off and removed the glossy mahogany box from the packaging.

I was touched at how he ran his fingers over the plaque, tracing the letters. "This is beautiful, Kara."

"It's a memory box for special things, like my Father's Day cards."

"Very nice, very, very nice," he said, seemingly unsure of exactly what to say. This was a man unused to showing his feelings, and I seemed to force the issue at every turn. . "Mrs. Schuster, come look at what Kara got me for Father's Day."

I began noticing that it was easier for him to show his feelings in the third person.

"Isn't that nice?" he said, again running his finger over the engraving.

"Oh wow, Governor, it's beautiful, and very special," she answered looking at me with a knowing that this was a big deal.

"I'm glad you like it...Dad." I felt my face grow warm. We hugged, and I could feel his gratitude in my own heart. Even though he didn't say much, I watched his eyes widen looking at the word *Dad*.

"Thank you, Kara, this is such a wonderful gift. Really — thank you very much."

After holding the box on his lap for a long time, he carefully placed it in a prominent place on the coffee table in his study. We finished our Father's Day with some of our favorite Oreos and milk, and I snuggled in the nook of his arm, soaking up the warmth and safety I always felt when having cookies with Dad. I was the only one of his children in town to share the day, and I was happy to be the one to honor him for becoming the great father it seemed he wanted to be.

After I gave my father the "Dad" box, I was excited to see Trooper Al Pontarelli so I could call my father Dad in front of him. When he came to pick up my father for work, I showed him the box, now a solid symbol of the new phase in our relationship.

"Good girl," he said.

Dad got a big redo on fatherhood with me. He had made mistakes by not always making things special for my brothers, but with each special occasion, I was teaching him how to show his heart. As I taught him how I needed to be loved, he learned how to show love to my brothers, too. As the years went on, I think he tried to make up for his mistakes with them by showing up for Tracy's races, doing a business deal with Stuart, or taking Hunter, Peter's son, to see a B-17 when it came to town. I learned he was just as hard on himself as anyone else could be, and he needed to feel unconditional love before he felt safe enough to open his heart. Somehow, my key worked. I'd unlocked a part of him that he'd needed to find, all the while discovering my true identity in the process.

14 Chip Off the New Block

Not only did I start calling my father Dad, but we started treating each other more like family as the glue of our relationship started to harden. Our newfound acceptance of each other made my second summer in Newport much calmer. The story of us reuniting was old news. Now the focus was on his bid for re-election.

His campaign for a third term was in full swing, and it was an uphill battle. He had promised the voters he would only seek two terms, but had changed his mind when his first term was consumed by the banking crisis that crippled the state. He felt he needed more time to accomplish his goals. At seventy-five, he was the nation's oldest governor, and under his tenure the governor's term was changed from two years to four, which meant he would have left office at age seventy-nine. Many thought that was just too old. Others didn't like the whiplash-like changes he brought about, like building a new expensive airport terminal, and revitalizing the city of Providence with big development projects. Today, the public has embraced those changes, and even named the airport terminal after my dad, along with a plaque inside thanking him for swimming against the tides of political opposition.

Back then though, the polls didn't look good, and his advisors didn't think he should run again. But there was no changing his mind. My friend, Dayna, came out to visit again, and we helped by making calls to prospective voters to get the word out. When my father stopped by and asked how it was going, I didn't want to tell him that two people had hung up on me when I mentioned his name. I didn't want to upset him, and I was having a great time going to debate preps and being by his side at campaign events.

One of those events is the V-J Day celebration. Rhode Island is the only state to celebrate Victory Over Japan Day as a state holiday in August, and everyone goes to the beach. So Dad and I headed to back to Narragansett for some hand shaking on the sand. I encouraged him to lose his blazer so he could fit in with the folks basking in the sun. I also dusted a little of my bronzing powder on his face.

"Wait...what's that?"

"It'll make you look less tired and more youthful," I said.

"Is that so," he answered, rolling his eyes.

As we trudged in our street clothes through the hot sand, we were stopped by the legendary political reporter, M. Charles Bakst, who'd carried on a love-hate relationship with my father in the paper. "Governor, did you go on vacation recently?"

"No, Charlie, I most certainly did not," my father shot back.

"You look like you have a good tan."

My father gave me a look, and I knew to keep quiet. It wouldn't go over well if I chimed in to say that I'd put my make-up on him. Obviously, my idea of helping him look rested didn't go over well. When Charlie was done with his badgering, Dad and I finished our hand shaking on the sand and made it back to the car. Once the doors were shut we cracked up as I told the trooper how I had just accidentally made my father look like a lazy sun worshipper with my favorite beauty fixer. Regardless of the tough polls, Dad and I were having a blast, and his approval ratings with me were sky high.

My boyfriend, Doug, came out to visit, and I felt my old nerves cropping up again, since this would be the first time I'd brought a guy home to meet Dad. I really wanted him to approve. If he didn't, well, I knew Doug might not last much longer. At that point in my life, everything orbited around my father. Since I'd missed out on the whole "Daddy's little girl," I was playing the part now.

Doug arrived, and I was relieved to see he was wearing a collared shirt, since I knew Dad would be judging. Whew, crisis #1 averted.

"Governor, it's nice to meet you. I'm Doug, and I wanted to thank you for having me to your beautiful home."

So far so good, he's using his manners. Ding!

"Nice to see you. Kara has spoken highly of you." A sudden thought popped into his head. "Listen, why don't you come to my debate preps tonight."

Yes! Doug had passed the sniff test.

"I'd love to," Doug answered, glancing at me with a smile.

Everything was going so well until my father let Doug drive home that night. They arrived at the toll booth at the Newport Bridge in the rain and Doug tried to toss the token in the basket, but missed. He had to get out of the car, find the token on the ground, and try again, all while my father was impatiently waiting and watching. I felt terrible for him, but also worried my athlete father would somehow hold this klutzy move against him.

He finally managed to get the job done, but for some reason my father kept calling him Chuck the rest of the weekend. He just couldn't get his name right, and as nice as Doug was, the relationship eventually fizzled. We weren't the best fit for each other anyway, but I realized then and there that I would need a guy who could handle my father and gain his respect.

As summer came to a close, I got ready to head back to school. This time my father was sending me back with a parting gift—his old Jeep he'd used to pull horses at the Virginia farm. He'd sold the farm to finance his campaign, and wanted me to have a car at school so I could get to my job as a waitress, and any internships I hoped to land. I wasn't sure where I was going to park a giant Wagoneer with a salamander hood ornament, which signified his code name in the Underground (so named because salamanders walk through fire), but I was grateful, nonetheless.

"Thank you, Dad," I said, giving him a huge hug. "This will help so much, especially when we get a foot of snow and I have to make it across campus for class."

"You're welcome, but I have some ground rules for your drive back to Michigan."

"Okay."

"I want to see the route you're taking on the map, and you are to call me every time you enter a new state. That way, if something happens, I know which state police to call."

"Will do, thank you." I stifled the urge to smile.

I loved that he was being overprotective. When he showed worry, I felt his love, and I was more than happy to abide by any rules. Some young college girls may have rolled their yes, but I craved his protection. Growing up, I had done so much of the worrying, and I often felt like I needed to be an adult to help my mom. Once, when she fell on hard times, the leasing company sent a man to repossess her car, and I ran outside and begged him not to take it. It didn't work, and he towed it away, and I felt so defeated and scared about what we would do to get around. Mom managed to make things work, as she always did, and got us another car, but the residue of worry from days like that still clogged my system. I loved having a father who could not only give me a car, but make me feel safe in it. He even gave me a cell phone, which was a luxury in 1994, and I promised to only use it in case of an emergency.

As I headed back to school, I followed my father's orders and called at every state border, hearing his deep voice answer the phone.

"Hi, it's me in New York."

"Thank you. Good job, call me in the next state."

As I headed back to school, I called almost daily to keep up with the campaign. When primary night came, I kept that cell phone by my side. The large brick-like contraption started ringing at 7:30 p.m., and I knew it was him. It was early, and that couldn't be good. I flipped open the phone. "Hi, Dad, how's it going?"

"We didn't win. We lost to Myrth York." His voice sounded heavy and defeated. "It's okay, we fought a good fight, and that's all we could do."

I could tell he was crushed. Out of every job he had ever had, being governor paid him the least, but he loved it the most.

My heart fell. "Oh, Dad, I'm so sorry. You should have won."

"Okay then, just wanted you to know," he said, clearly needing to get off the phone.

I could tell he didn't want to say anything more, but I wanted him to know I could feel his pain and disappointment. "Love you," I said softly.

"Love to you as well, have a good night," he said as he hung up. Saying I love you was still hard for him, but that would come in time.

I knew this loss would be tough on Dad because he still had so many things he wanted to accomplish. I knew the articles the next day must have stung his tough skin, reporting that he became the first incumbent Governor in the history of the state to lose in a primary. It was another extreme for Dad, elected in the largest landslide in state history and voted out for the record books, as well.

I worried about what my father would do once he left office. He'd always said that retirement is a terminal illness, but I hoped having more free time meant I'd see more of him. He was going to be seventy-five years old, and I wanted him to slow down and take care of himself so I could have him as long as possible. I was racing the clock trying to make up for lost time, so I made every effort to be with him when I was off school. We spent another glorious family vacation at my father's house in Jamaica. While we all had lots of laughs and fun, it was also a bittersweet time because we knew the end of vacation meant that Dad wouldn't be the governor anymore.

As he left office, I elected to follow in my father's footsteps as a chip off the new block as a Political Science and Communications major. I needed to get some real world experience, so I started searching for summer internships, and decided I wanted to work at the White House and CNN's Washington Bureau.

I knew I was aiming high, but I filled out the applications for the internships and began collecting letters of recommendation from my professors and some politicians I'd met through Dad. My name was still Kara Hewes, so I had a degree of anonymity.

After about two months, I got a letter from the White House saying I had been accepted to the summer internship program. I jumped up and down and ran to my phone to call my father. "Dad, I have incredible news!"

"What?"

"I am going to be an intern at the White House this summer!"

There was a long pause.

"That's great, how did that happen?"

"I applied for it," I said, feeling very proud of myself.

"Good for you! Good for you!" It warmed my heart to hear him banging his hand on his desk in excitement.

But the thrills didn't stop there. A few days later, I got another letter saying I had also been accepted to the CNN internship program.

Dad was equally thrilled. "I just read an article about Christiane Amanpour, and it says she is a hard worker and not a name dropper. She's someone for you to follow."

This was his way of telling me he was proud I'd done it all on my own. Though I had inherited a father who could open many doors, I still wanted to do the knocking myself.

"Nice work, I'm going to call up my ex-wives who live in Washington, Joy and Pammy, so we can get you some help down there."

"Really? Okay thanks, Dad, that sounds great. But are you sure they would want to meet me?" It seemed strange that he thought it was okay to call up his ex-wives, especially Joy, since she was the one he cheated on with my mother. Why would she want to show me around?

"Believe it or not, Joy and I are still dear friends—it's no problem. She's a former CIA agent, so you should get to know her."

My father was full of surprises—who knew he was married to a CIA agent?

Obviously, Dad didn't have the usual relationships one would expect with an ex-wife, and he was right; Joy said she'd be happy to have me over to dinner when I arrived in town, and even introduced me to some people she thought I should know. More predictably, Pammy never got back to him.

To this day, I remain so happy that Joy welcomed me into her home when I arrived that summer. We never talked about how I was a product of a hurtful part of her marriage. Instead, she told me stories of how she helped get Mikhail Baryshnikov out of Russia.

She also introduced me to her daughter, Cintra, who became like a big sister to me. Cintra was ten years my senior, and I idolized her. She was a tall, head-turning blonde with exquisite taste and bold personality. Like my father, she could fill a room, and she wasn't afraid to speak her mind, even to my dad. Her father had died, and she had spent her formative years under my father's roof. When she took me out on the town in DC, she regaled me with stories about growing up with him. It gave me a window into what I had missed, even if it wasn't all pretty. My father was tough and not around a lot and, like me, she felt like she did a lot of growing up on her own. But we also shared a love for him and the same ability to see the good in him.

And I was about to witness some of that good when Dad surprised me, yet again.

As if calling his ex-wives wasn't shocking enough, Dad really pulled the rabbit out of the hat when he called me unexpectedly. As usual, his tone was brief and to the point. "Do you want a blue car or a grey car?"

I was in the middle of studying for a test, so this caught me flat-footed. "What do you mean?"

"Really, what do you care so long as you get a new car, right?" He seemed to be talking to himself. "A car...you'll need one in Washington."

"Blue," I replied, matching his brevity.

Click.

Summer arrived a few weeks later, and I arrived at Dad's house for a quick visit before going to DC. He took me to the Herb Chambers car dealership, and inside was a blue Mazda with a red bow on it. I nearly cried. This was another turning point for me, and I stopped to think about all I'd wished for—the dream of finding Dad—and here I was, watching my father's wide grin splash across his face while I drove out of the car dealership. Even though he was still uncertain about what life after the governorship would be like, he was excited to help me begin my budding career—and in the same place he started his, no less. It seemed ironic—or was it DNA?—that thirty-some years after he served with President Kennedy, I would go to work for another president, even if I was just answering phones and doing data entry. Nonetheless, Dad was so proud, and told everyone he knew that his daughter was going to be a White House intern. I was also proud to be one of only 225 interns selected from a pool of thousands of applicants from across the country. Little did I know that we would be the class most known for one now-infamous intern, Monica Lewinsky.

Though I never met her, I did get to meet President Clinton, twice, and when I told him who my father was, he shook my hand and said, "Governor Sundlun is a great American, and we're grateful for his service."

During my father's time in office, he was the only Jewish governor in America, and had traveled with President Clinton to

Israel for peace talks.

I beamed with pride, and found myself wanting to work harder to achieve great things like Dad.

My internship at CNN was equally life changing for me. It was there that I knew I wanted to become a news reporter. I loved seeing the inner workings of the White House, but my stint at CNN convinced me I wanted to be the one reporting on the action, not working behind the scenes. Larry King's speech to us interns was simple: "Don't worry about the competition. If you're good, you'll get a good job."

I was determined to get good.

One of my jobs was helping deliver scripts to Judy Woodruff, the anchor for *Inside Politics*. She knew of my desire to get into the industry, and helped me craft a news story on welfare reform for my resume tape. On my off day, I went out to the Capitol in my red suit to shoot what's called a "stand up" for my story. I made sure my make-up was good and used the extra strong Aussie hairspray to form the requisite TV helmet hair. The weather was perfect, and the photographer thought my script was good, but something kept gnawing at me as I said, "Live in Washington, I'm Kara Hewes."

I knew I needed to change my name. Hewes was connected to a man who'd had no meaning to me for many years. I wanted to be Sundlun. I wanted to really be my father's daughter in name, as well as our shared DNA, and I needed to make the change before I started sending out my resumes for a job. Problem was, I didn't know how to ask my father. I figured I'd think of some way to ask him during my summer internships, but it would take me until senior year before I had enough guts to bring it up.

In the meantime, my junior year began with my father deciding to come out for Parents' Weekend. I couldn't wait to introduce him to all my friends and show him my life at the university. Mom was also coming, and I worried how the two of them would behave with all the togetherness of walking around campus, going to the football game, and meeting my friends. I feared the awkwardness, but yearned for the normalcy of two parents supporting me, even if they had a very storied past.

Mom arrived first, wearing something entirely too dressy for a football game. Her hair and makeup were perfect, and it was clear she wanted to look her best when she met Dad. However, I wondered if all the glitz would survive Michigan Stadium—The Big House—the largest football stadium in the country.

Dad arrived wearing his trademark grey slacks and a navy blazer, which was a giant contrast to all the other dads who sported jeans and Wolverine sweatshirts, not to mention that he was old enough to be their father. Both Mom and Dad exchanged pleasantries and an awkward hug. Surreal didn't even touch what I was thinking.

Later, wearing the University of Michigan sweatshirts I'd bought them, Mom and Dad met my friends and their parents. Dad was at least thirty-five years older than my friends' parents, but it didn't faze him at all. It didn't take him more than a few minutes to strike up a conversation and assume his natural position of holding court. While I went searching for some drinks for my parents, I could see my father telling a story while Mom and the other parents listened intently. I had the continued urge to pinch myself just to make sure I wasn't dreaming.

Dad loved football, and was excited, especially since he'd never seen a Big Ten game—and if he had, he would have avoided sitting in the student section. "Bunch of rogues," he said, laughing while picking a poorly aimed marshmallow out of his hair. "Don't they sit down in Michigan?"

"Not in the student section," I laughed back.

"Times have really changed. When I was in college, we wore a suit and tie and the ladies wore fur coats, and you always went with a date."

"Yep, times have definitely changed—we have cars now, too."

Even though I knew Mom didn't know a lick about football

and was probably bored out of her mind, I loved the idea of enjoying this as a family. When the day was done, Mom was tired from the emotional day, and decided to head home. Dad gave her a goodbye peck on the cheek, which made her beam from ear to ear—it was so apparent to me that she still loved him on some level.

But Dad wanted to stick around, and offered to take the girls and me out to dinner. The timing was perfect, since I was looking forward to showing him off to my new friends without having to worry about making Mom feel uncomfortable.

The restaurant was known for its quiet atmosphere, charming antique décor, and five star food—the kind of place you only go when someone's parents are in town to pick up the tab! Our table was perfect, and Dad was happy to be surrounded with me and my roommates, Heather, Laura, Lauren, and Jenny. I loved how my friends seemed so enamored with his stories.

For the first time, I was getting to show Dad *my* turf. I had always gone to my dad's world, which was off in another galaxy, away from my real life. Now I was getting him to land on Planet Kara, and I wanted him to see the other side of me.

The girls were entranced as Dad explained why he became a Democrat, even though his father, Walter, my grandfather, had run for the senate in Rhode Island as a Republican.

"I was an intern for President Roosevelt," Dad said in a tone suggesting we should all be impressed by his connection to such a historic figure.

Laura could help but crack a joke that left us all in tears, "T.R. or F.D.R.?"

"Very funny," my father jibed back.

While everyone laughed, I looked around the table and smiled to myself. My dad. Here. In my life. At my university. Joking with my friends. Amazing and priceless.

Being around my father and hearing about his adventures got me interested in seeing the world. As a junior, I'd decided it might be a great idea to spend a semester abroad and solidify my years of

Spanish classes, but I was a little nervous to ask my dad if I could go. My friends, Laura and Jenny, had already signed up for a program in Seville, Spain, and it didn't look like there would be any cost difference in tuition. But, once again, I was shackled by that fear that going abroad was not in our legal agreement. Even though I knew our relationship was real now, I still worried about deviating from that piece of paper because it had triggered so much good. Application deadlines were approaching, so I knew I had to bite the bullet and call him.

"Hi Dad, um I have a question for you."

"Yes, go ahead, how can I help you?"

I was so nervous — how I hated asking for anything extra! — and the words just tumbled out of me in one breath. "Um, well, I really want to study abroad, and I really think it'll help me get a better job down the road. I mean, I already speak some Spanish, and I could probably become fluent."

"Will the university allow you to go?" He sounded genuinely interested, making me think he sort of liked the idea. *Yay!*

"Yes, they encourage it, actually. There's a program in Spain and another one called Semester at Sea where you can sail around the world and learn about many countries."

I wanted Spain, but felt like I should give all the options.

"No, Semester at Sea sounds like just a big party and all you'll end up with is a bunch of postcards. I'm not paying for that, but Spain is a beautiful country, and I have some great friends in Madrid I can call."

"Really?" I squeaked, not believing my ears. "So I can go?"

"I think it'd be good for you."

It was all I could do to keep from jumping on the furniture. "Ok, Dad, thank you so much! Thankyouthankyouthankyou!"

I rushed my applications and could barely contain my excitement to be going to Europe for the first time, where I would live with a Spanish family and take classes at the University of Sevilla. I left right after Christmas, using the brand new luggage Dad gave me to send me on my way in style.

The limits of our relationship were being lifted and, thanks to my dad, my life abroad expanded my worldview at the same time. He even helped me with extra expenses so I could stay longer and backpack around Europe before coming back to live with him for my fourth summer in Newport. Because of my time abroad, my Spanish is pretty good, and I often do recordings in Spanish for my television station today. *¡Gracias, papa!*

After Spain, I was able to spend a few weeks in Newport, sharing all of my adventures with Dad. It would be the last summer before I graduated college, and I was aware I needed to make these moments count, since I wouldn't be able to come home for weeks at a time once I started working.

As I headed back to the University of Michigan for my senior year, I was excited and looking forward to graduation. Not only did it mark the calendar of my fourth year of having Dad in my life, it was another milestone he could witness. But I knew I needed to change my name before I started sending out resumes for jobs, and I definitely didn't want "Kara Hewes" on my diploma. Still, a small sliver of me feared rejection again. What if he says no? What if he says that wasn't part of our deal? Our legal agreement only covered me until the end of college, so what if he wants to bail out?

It was crazy talk, I know, but I was still vulnerable to the old wounds of abandonment in times like this, where I felt I was going outside the bounds of our agreement. Should I just keep quiet, or ask him?

Our relationship is real and becoming so much more solid every day. Just ask him, Kara!

In the end, I listened to my heart.

Dad was now working at the University of Rhode Island for the Governor in Residence program, which was created to help URI make strategic partnerships and secure funding for expanding its programs. I called up his office and his sweet secretary, Cecelia, answered.

"Hi, Cecelia is my father in?" I felt my stomach tightening.

"Hey, baby," he boomed. Ah, good, his greeting meant he was in a good mood and happy to talk.

"Hi, Dad, how are you?"

"Good, how are you?"

"Fine, um I need to talk to you about something."

"What?"

"Well I'm putting my resume together to start applying for jobs after college, and there's a problem."

"What's the problem?"

"I don't want to use the last name Hewes anymore. I—I want to change it to Sundlun." Holding the phone away from my mouth, I let out a huge gasp, like a deflating balloon. *Breathe Kara, breathe.*

Dad's long pause didn't do my heart rate or blood pressure any good. Was he figuring out a reason to say no? Maybe he wasn't really ready to make me totally official. Wait…I knew he loved me, and wasn't everyone else telling me it was clear I'd changed his life for the better? I squashed the urge to kick myself.

"Well, how do we do that?" His voice oozed approval and— dare I say it—excitement.

Relief washed over me. Would my fear of rejection ever go away? Would I ever feel as secure as I did with Mom? I figured a name change would help make it even more real for both of us. It was a tangible way of erasing the past.

"Do we need a lawyer?"

He let out a small chuckle. "Kara, I *am* a pretty good lawyer, so I think I can handle a name change."

Even better! Dad would make himself mine, *and* do all the work. Another deposit of love to fill up my heart's savings account. Like a little girl who scribbles names of a boy she likes, I started practicing my new signature, Kara Kathleen Sundlun. Hey! All my father's monogrammed towels would work for me, too.

Dad went to probate court in Rhode Island and easily changed my name in less than an hour. *The Providence Journal* reported it the next day: "Kara takes her Dad's name." Seeing it in print made it feel even more real. Dad sent me the official documents so I could change my driver's license, credit card, and school records. I wanted to make sure I became Kara Sundlun before graduation, so the yearbook would have my new identity, and my diploma would reflect the new truth.

I was overjoyed that my past was being erased, but Mom wondered where she fit in. She watched my father take center stage as I became a young adult, and felt like she had been replaced as the star of my life.

The tears would well up in her big blue-green eyes. "Sometimes it just feels like you're choosing him over me, like I'm being discarded."

"Mom, you're my mother, and no one can ever take that away. Besides, it's not *your* name I'm replacing, and I'll always keep my middle name Kathleen, and will always be your little 'Kara Kathleen,' I said, using the same sing-songy voice she'd always used when calling me. While most mothers use both names when a kid is in trouble— mine sang my names like a song when she was happy.

As much as it hurt, she knew it didn't make sense for me to keep the name of her ex-husband, a man who reminded me of chipped plates at the dinner table. She ended up going back to her maiden name Vargo, and we both said goodbye to an unpleasant memory.

With my new name made official, I could graduate as a Sundlun in May of 1997, with my father; brother, Stuart; and Cousin Fenton there to cheer me on, along with Mom and my cousin, Danielle.

I reveled in having both sides of my family merging on this milestone. It had been nearly four years since we'd come together under the glare of television lights, and we now had a relationship that was far more real than any pundit could have predicted. This life moment was a major achievement for Dad and me. Against all odds, I'd found him, and we had found our way to each other. Officially, he had fulfilled his contractual agreement by paying for my college, but personally, our relationship was taking on a new beginning. From now on, if I wanted to attend grad school, get married, or buy a house, I would have to discuss my aspirations with my father, like any other normal kid.

Contractually, he no longer owed me anything, but we had grown beyond courtrooms and contracts. I knew he would be there for me because he *wanted* to. Forgiveness hadn't come easily, but I knew I'd made the right choice by letting go of the past. In doing so, we shared a father-daughter love that would be forever, and our road to healing would continue far past the date on my diploma, or our settlement agreement.

15 My First Job

A chip off the new block, I was following in my dad's footsteps and hoping to enter the exciting world of television news—only I wanted to be in front of the camera rather than being a star in the boardroom. Even with my family name, I knew it would all come down to my on-air resume tape.

I started working around the clock at WJBK in Detroit as an intern, trying to soak up all the experience I could from my mentor, investigative reporter Bill Gallagher. He was a wicked smart Irishman who knew how to get a story better than anyone, but also liked to enjoy life, so he never failed to find time for a good lunch and—since he knew I was working for free—he always paid for me, too. We usually worked with photographer Dave Mabry, who was helping me put my resume tape together.

After Bill did his story for the evening news, I would take the raw interviews and write my own stories, and Dave would help me shoot stand ups: "Live in Detroit, I'm Kara Sundlun." I loved saying my new name, even though it still felt awkward, and I continued having a hard time enunciating the "d."

I needed to put together a crackerjack tape to reflect my new name and maturity. The stuff I'd done when I interned in Rhode Island at seventeen wasn't going to get me a real job as a TV news reporter, and I didn't want to use my CNN stories that still had my old last name.

I sent out tapes of my work to dozens of stations across the country. In return, I got loads of rejection letters, or nothing at all. This was a cutthroat business, and I quickly learned that it didn't

matter who your dad was if you weren't what the news
director wanted.

After months of searching, and hundreds of dollars in
postage and VHS tapes, I landed a job in the tiny town of
Charlottesville, Virginia, home to the University of Virginia.
Out of about two hundred TV markets in America,
Charlottesville was market 196. It was a far cry from the
network news job I aspired to, but I was grateful for their offer,
since I knew they had hundreds of tapes from wannabe
reporters. Dave Cupp—news director and evening anchor—
decided he liked me enough to offer me an entry level reporter
job for $18,000 dollars a year. I felt like I'd won the lottery, and
couldn't wait to tell Dad.

"Dad, I got the job!"

"Good for you! I know Charlottesville well, you'll love it
there. It's not far from great horse country." Too bad he had
sold the farm. It was only a couple hours away and would have
been a perfect weekend respite when I needed a break from
beans and rice, which was all I was going to be able to afford.

Even though I was only going to be a cub reporter, it felt
cool to be following in Dad's general footsteps. I drove to
Rhode Island first and loaded up a U-Haul with furniture Dad
gave me from his garage. I had an antique highboy, horse hair
chaise lounge, and dozens of monogrammed placemats. He
even threw in some pieces of silver.

My new decor clashed with my humble salary, but I liked
eating noodles on dinnerware fit for nobility.

During my first week on the job, Dad called the newsroom
frantically looking for me. The assignment editor who took the
call came rushing over to my desk. "Kara, Governor Sundlun is
on the phone for you..."

I could see him suddenly connecting the dots...my last
name, the Governor...and I realized any anonymity I'd enjoyed
as a regular gal was blown. But by now, I was used to Dad
making himself known.

Ever impatient, he dove right in with little preamble. "Kara, I've been looking all over for you, and I couldn't get your number from the operator. They say it's unlisted."

"It is, Dad, that's why I had you write it down. It's not safe for a young woman on TV to list her address and phone number."

The exasperation in his voice grew. "What kind of news reporter are you? Emergencies happen on weekends and holidays, so how is anyone ever going to find you?"

I tried not to laugh. "Dad, trust me, I'll do fine. The station can always get hold of me."

A few days later he called back to admit he'd been wrong to blow his top. "I called Karen Adams at Channel 12 in Providence who, by the way, is someone you should aspire to be, really a first rate news anchor. Anyway, she agreed that you shouldn't list your number, so I'll yield to her advice."

My father's antics never angered me because his concern was the grounding force I had always needed in my life. Mom's effervescence sometimes meant living life in the clouds, which translated to not knowing when, where, or how to land. By contrast, Dad's tight tether on me made me feel steady and safe. I needed both energies to feel balanced.

As much as Dad tried to keep his finger on my pulse, I had big plans to conquer the world of TV news. Being the next big name as a war correspondent or network anchor danced through my head. However, it didn't take long for my delusions of grandeur to crash and burn. After only two weeks on the job, I was working on a Sunday morning and heard "murder/suicide, Commonwealth Ave." on the police scanner. Since this was Tiny Town, USA, I was a one woman band, shooting, writing, and editing my own stories.

I grabbed a map and rushed to the scene, cursing my horrible sense of direction. When I arrived, I was the only reporter on the scene. A man had shot his girlfriend and turned the gun on himself, leaving their two-year-old baby crying in the crib. The woman's family was understandably distraught and yelling profanities at me as I tried to get footage from a safe distance, hoping the camera was straight. The teenaged sister of the victim came rushing at me and shoved the camera into my face. It fell to the ground with a loud cracking sound. Watching it splinter into several pieces, I thought my whole career had splintered with it because I knew the camera cost more than a family car. The police rushed over to grab the girl before she could do anything else, but it was clear my eye was already swelling and developing a black and blue ring around it. I decided I'd better call my news director, Dave Cupp, and let him know what happened. Dave calmly asked if I was okay before sending in a photographer with a truck, so I could report live from the scene. I had never done a live shot before and wanted to tell him about my black eye, but I decided I'd try to cover it up with some makeup, since this could be my big break.

Well, so much for my big break. So much for Dad's great genes. It was absolutely awful. I gave a terrible, shaky, jumbled report. My voice was irritatingly high, I couldn't keep the facts straight, and I even messed up signing off. I was so nervous, I said "Live in Charlottesville," when it was really Albemarle County, the kind of mistake that would make any local think you were an idiot. I was so upset with myself, Dave's disappointment felt like nothing. Thankfully, he didn't fire me, and instead put me on easier fluff stories and had me help out with data entry in his office.

My very wise talent agent, Steve Dickstein, had always told me that you want to make your mistakes in a place where no one is watching, so you don't offend your future employers. I was learning that my lineage didn't matter, I would still be judged on what I produced, regardless of my fancy new last name. In some ways the name was a curse because people had greater expectations of me, so starting from a false pedestal ensured that I had farther to fall. Fortunately, my determination muscle was already strong, and I overcame my image of being too green by working hard. I had already seen how persistence paid off when I was trying to get Dad to accept me, so I used the same strategies to convince my employers I could get better. And I did. I started breaking big stories in town and took voice lessons to learn how to sound more authoritative. I spent weekends in writing workshops polishing my craft and, after about fourteen months it paid off. I got a job offer from Grand Rapids-Battle Creek Michigan, market thirty eight, which was about a 160 market jump!

This time, I was ready. I got an apartment next to the police station and worked day and night developing sources and breaking stories. My drive was, in part, fueled by a deep need to make it to an even bigger market on the East Coast, so I could be closer to Dad. He was nearing eighty, and I felt like I was racing the clock. I wanted to see him as much as possible, but I also wanted to grow a great career. Part of me thought about just quitting TV and living with Dad while I got some sort of job to pay my bills, but I felt like that would be selling out. I now had two dreams, building a relationship with my father and a solid career that would make both of us proud. While I was in Michigan, I covered some big stories and got to interview presidential candidates like John McCain, since they all campaigned often in our swing state.

I loved sharing the stories with Dad as a way to bond over his love of politics. I was also starting to tell Dad more about the new beau in my life, whom he knew very, very well. David, the staffer who picked me up at the airport the first day I met my father, was now my boyfriend. We'd reconnected on a reunion trip for my father's old staff. I knew my father loved him, and that meant the world to me.

"You know he's actually known me longer than you have," I teased my father.

My father loved having him around. "He's a good young man."

And it didn't hurt that David still called him Governor! It felt good to have a man in my life who understood our complicated history without my having to explain anything. We dated for a few years and had a wonderful time, but eventually went our separate ways.

I wasn't the only one who had gone separate ways: Dad delivered his own breaking news. After being married to Marjorie for a little over a decade, he'd decided to divorce her and marry Soozie, the woman he'd been secretly dating for years. Dad promised he would always take care of Marjorie—and he did— since she wasn't self-sufficient after her accident.

"We are madly in love," Dad said about Soozie.

It would be my father's 5th wedding, and my brothers joked that each time the women kept getting younger. Soozie was only forty-six years old, thirty-four years younger than my father.

I didn't know what to say. It's not that I didn't know about Soozie, because I did, but I always felt guilty about knowing. She was a photographer, and they'd met while she was taking his picture—years before I surfaced. Eventually, he introduced us, and I liked her.

She was a beautiful, talented, loving mother of two wonderful children a little younger than me. Though they'd been together for years, I never thought he'd marry her. He had always insisted that he would never leave Marjorie because of the accident. It made it doubly hard because Marjorie had been so nice to me. I wondered if I should just be happy for Dad and Soozie. After all, what were my choices? I mean, I could stamp my feet, but that wouldn't change the outcome. Facts were, he loved her and she loved him, so wasn't that enough? Marjorie would be taken care of, so do I need to worry about something I can't control? There were no easy answers, and all I could do was look to my brothers for guidance on how to handle this news.

Tracy wasn't thrilled, but he wasn't exactly surprised either. "Dad is Dad—this is what he's been doing all his life. He did it to our mother and every wife after."

"I really like Soozie, and I know how happy she makes him, but I just feel bad for Marjorie."

This wasn't easy. My dad had become my hero, yet he was far from perfect. I could either judge him and lose him, or love him in spite of his imperfections. My brothers had far more experience with this, and their attitude was that step-families come and go—it was part of life with Dad.

I didn't want to think of my father as the "womanizer" the papers referred to, but I also didn't think it was my place to intervene, especially since my brothers' experiences had taught them to take the news in stride.

Dad planned to marry Soozie at his home in Jamaica, and he expected us all to be there. "We're getting married on January 1, 2000, and we want you all to be in the wedding party."

"Wow, that's great, let me see what I can do about work."

Uh-oh was the first thought that came to mind, since we were staring down the gun barrel of the infamous Y2K, and everyone feared computer systems around the world might crash. My station had already informed everyone that no one would be getting New Year's off this year—no exceptions. I was afraid asking about going to my father's wedding would be career suicide, but I knew I had to push. I'd missed so many events with my father, and I didn't want to miss this. After a few tense conversations, my boss relented and I promised if Y2K did corrupt the world, I could do reports from Jamaica, making our coverage look even more expansive. I don't think he bought into it, but he was clearly sick of my asking, and finally gave in.

Soozie wanted my brothers and me, along with her two grown children, Max and Heather, to make up the wedding party. We wore dresses in her favorite shade of blue, while Dad and Soozie were pronounced man and wife under one of the most beautiful sunsets I'd ever seen. I couldn't help but stand back and look at everyone and marvel that we really had become a family. Dad had made it a point to include me, insisting that I attend and be a bridesmaid. I loved sharing another special moment with him, since we had missed so many. As usual, I didn't want my time with my father to end, and I couldn't wait for the next family gathering.

As a footnote—and I know this is going to be hard to believe—Marjorie and Dad remained close, even after the wedding. He helped her get a nice apartment that offered assisted living, and when it came time for Soozie to host her first Sundlun Family Thanksgiving, she warmly invited Marjorie…and my mother. Shocker, I know. What's even more bizarre is they both responded to the formal invitations with a yes! I didn't know what was stranger—having my mother and father celebrate Thanksgiving together, or watch my father dine with his ex-girlfriend, ex-wife, and his new wife like nothing ever happened. Soozie made sure to snap the only picture I have of me and my parents sharing a holiday, and it's framed in my home today. I had always dreamed of normal, and this decidedly didn't qualify—but in a way it was better. We were a real family and, despite our many flaws, we all decided to love each other anyway. That was something to truly be grateful for.

I returned to my job in Michigan depressed. It was hard being so far away from Dad, and I worked hard to find a job opening closer to him. I'd sent out tapes, but no one was biting.

Finally, an exciting offer from WTAE in Pittsburgh came through, and my agent advised me to take the wonderful opportunity. It was tempting—a great station in a bigger market—but it was still a plane ride away from my father, and I couldn't bring myself to commit. It was a hard decision, but soon after that, I received an offer for a part-time job in Hartford, Connecticut. My agent thought the Pittsburgh job was clearly the better choice, with its bigger market, more money, and full time. But I chose Hartford because it was only a two hour drive from Dad. I figured I needed one more good job before I could break into New York or Boston, and thought Hartford would be good enough. And the upside was that I could go home to Dad every weekend if I wanted. My heart was leading the way, so a bigger paycheck and more prestige would have to wait. Little did I know seven years after meeting my father, I would meet the man I was going to marry at that television station in Hartford. Seems the Universe was guiding me again.

16 Dad Signs Off on the One

Dennis House was one of the first people I met at my new station. He was handsome with dark hair that was always disheveled until moments before the newscast, and copper colored eyes. But it was his boyish demeanor that instantly disarmed me. He smiled broadly, making his dimples pop, and introduced himself in his deep, warm voice, "Hi, Kara, I'm Dennis, welcome to Channel Three."

I felt my face blush as I thanked him. One of the main anchors excited to meet me? I wished I'd have thought of something cleverer to say.

Dennis was only in his mid-thirties, which was quite young to be one of the main evening anchors at WFSB, one of the most-watched CBS affiliates in the country. I was a bit intimidated on my first day, since some of the biggest names in the business, like Gayle King, Bill O'Reilly, and Mika Brzezinski, had come out of WFSB. But Dennis put me at ease by joking that he'd been waiting to meet me, especially after reading my bio. Obviously, it wasn't because I'd broken some huge story. Come to find out, we'd both interned at WPRI in Providence, then worked in the Grand Rapids market before ending up in Hartford. It was fate that Dennis also loved Newport, and had a beach cottage there.

We became instant friends, but I was leery of anything more since I knew it wasn't smart to become the "anchor's girlfriend." I harkened back to what Dad always told me: "In the military, they taught us to keep it five hundred yards from the flagpole," meaning keep your love life off base!

Instead, we became good friends, and I loved being around him. I kept true to keeping it five hundred yards from the flagpole, but Mom helped change the course of our relationship when she came to visit me. Dennis and I had gone to the gym together and were doing a little grocery shopping when we bumped into her. She had heard about Dennis, but when she saw us sharing a cart, her Hungarian vibes kicked in, and she pulled Dennis aside and whispered something in his ear.

"Mom! What are you doing?" I was more than a little annoyed and embarrassed.

"Nothing...just being your mother," she answered cryptically, while Dennis had a broad smile splashed across his face.

That night Dennis decided to go for it and kissed me for the first time, confessing what my mother had told him: "Hang in there, you're the one for her."

The kiss was great, but I was still worried that we both worked together. Mom was never one for being practical, and encouraged me to follow my heart on this one. She loved to be nosy, and insisted she knew Dennis would be the man I would marry, after just taking one look at him. She must have been clairvoyant, because it wouldn't take me long to forget about the fact that our paychecks came from the same place.

Despite Mom's eagerness about Dennis, I refrained from telling my father about him, assuming he wouldn't like that I broke the flagpole rule. Then one night fellow reporter Kim Fettig and I stopped by Dennis's Newport cottage for a drink. I told him we couldn't stay long since Kim and I were having dinner with my father at the Skybar in Newport. Little did I know that Dennis took that morsel of information as invitation to meet my father. When I left him, he was wearing shorts and a baseball cap, and still grimy from a day at the beach. Thirty minutes later, Kim spotted him first at the top of the stairs walking into the exclusive restaurant dressed like Gatsby himself in a summer khaki suit and blue and white striped tie.

Kim leaned over and whispered to me. "Kara, I think that's Dennis over there."

"What....oh my God, it is. What's he doing here?"

With an air of confidence, Dennis walked up to our table and went straight to my father, without even glancing at me. "Governor, I'm Dennis House."

Dad looked at him incredulously. "You're the anchorman?" he asked, arching an eyebrow.

"Among other things," Dennis answered somewhat cryptically.

"It's the other things I'm worried about!" Dad shot back, cracking us up.

He invited Dennis to join us, and spent the rest of the evening asking him loads of questions: where was he from, how did he get his start in the business, and how was I doing at the station.

Let's face it, it was an interrogation, but Dennis loved it. Seeing these two become fast friends was huge for me, and my respect for Dennis grew because he realized how important my father was to me.

Two months later, the terror attacks on 9-11 changed Dennis's and my relationship forever. Suddenly, life felt too precious to worry about dating a guy who shared a boss with me. Though we didn't say it then, we knew we'd never be apart again. We covered the tragedy together for about ten days in New York City.

The attacks were frightening on a personal level as well. Dad was supposed to be at a meeting at the Pentagon, where one of the planes had hit. Fortunately, the meeting had been moved, and my father was safe and on his way back home. The few moments of panic reminded me how terrified I was of losing him before we got to say all that needed to be said. I'd finally found him, and there was so much lost time to make up for. I needed him to be there to walk me down the aisle, watch me have kids, and simply cherish the father-daughter time we'd both missed.

One of those father-daughter moments happened in the spring of 2002, about seven months after the 9-11 attacks, when I was nominated for my first Emmy Award for news reporting. I never expected to win, but nonetheless, I invited my father to be my date for the ceremony, thinking it would be fun to have him share in my excitement. Dennis had also been nominated, so I felt like we were keeping it in the family. The New England Emmy Awards dinner was in Dennis's hometown of Boston, and reporters from all over New England were there, including some from Providence who had covered Dad while he was Governor. They stopped by to shake hands with him, but he made it a point to tell them this was my night in the lights. "This is my daughter, Kara, she's nominated tonight."

When the ceremony started, Dad focused intently on the program, making notes of who won each Emmy, eagerly waiting for my category, which was toward the end. When the emcees started to announce General Assignment News, I sat nervously looking at Dad and Dennis. "Good Luck" they mouthed to me. There were reporters there with far more experience than I had, so it was a thrill just to be nominated.

"...And the Emmy goes to Kara Sundlun...for 'Swimming with Sharks.' "

The announcers went on to read the names of our talented photographer, Eric Budney, and gifted editor, Tom Zukowski, who worked on the piece with me. The country had been riveted by an increase in shark attacks down south, so we'd chartered a boat and chummed the waters with blood and fish guts to reveal what kind of sharks were swimming in New England waters. The day of the shoot I ended up getting sea sick and losing my breakfast over the side of the boat.

A similar feeling seized me as I stood to walk up to the stage, suddenly realizing I'd have to speak and hadn't prepared any remarks. Thankfully, Eric and Tom walked up to the stage with me, which calmed my shaking knees. But since I'd been the one who'd worked on camera, they left the speaking to me. I pulled myself together and thanked Eric and Tom, and, of course, the station. I took a deep breath and looked out into the crowd. "I want to thank my parents, especially my dad who is here tonight. I am so happy we can share this moment together."

Dad was so excited about my win he couldn't wait to start making phone calls to share the news. Dad, the master of embellishment, had a great time telling everyone I'd won an Emmy for being the "Best News Reporter in New England." Oops.

The idea of my dad bragging about my accomplishments had been a lifelong dream that I'd carried—even when there had been nothing in my life to suggest such a thing would actually happen.

Dreams really do come true.

17 Walking Me Down the Aisle

Spring, 2002

Though I knew I'd marry Dennis someday, I didn't know when. Laura, one of my best friends from college was the first in our group to get engaged, and we decided to take a girls' trip to Paris to celebrate. Sounds fancy, I know, but that's Laura, and since we were all young and single, taking a trip was no big deal. While I was away, Dennis decided to ask my father if he could come and see him. Dad had no experience with future sons-in-law asking for daughters' hands in marriage, so he was beyond excited when Dennis asked him for his blessing, and immediately asked Soozie to break out some champagne to celebrate.

While they toasted Dennis's big decision, my father wanted to offer some advice. Dennis figured it would be some sage wisdom considering my father had been married five times. But no. Instead, Dad said, "Dennis, when women get married they tend to gain weight, and Kara is short, so she won't carry it well. You'll really have to watch what she eats."

Dennis was so flabbergasted, he managed to mumble out a tepid "oh, um, okay," while thinking, a*nd this is why he's been married five times!*

Dennis was afraid I'd be ticked off, and waited a long time before telling me that story. But I just cracked up because my father was given to brutal honesty with his sometimes bizarre opinions, no matter how inappropriate. Dennis's relationship with his own father had been strained, so he enjoyed my father's eagerness to embrace him as family. Dad was always happy to share his thoughts with Den on politics and, of course, offer plenty of advice on just about everything—from what he should do to advance his career to how he should cut his hair, or what kind of pants to wear. So it seemed only fitting, that Dennis decided to buy my engagement ring from my father's jeweler, a man named Angel, at the Platinum House in Newport. But, still needing to be his own man, Dennis did it in secret before he asked for Dad's blessing. Guess he was pretty confident he'd get a yes!

Den still had a napkin drawing I'd made a month ago, when he'd surreptitiously asked what kind of ring I'd want "if" I was to get married, and took it to Angel.

When it came time to pop the question Dennis arranged an elaborate scheme to get me to Michigan because of its significance— I'd grown up there, he'd worked there and, most importantly, he was also thinking of my mom, and knew it would mean the world to her since he knew our wedding would be in Newport, on Dad's territory. Since Den loved producing big moments, he popped the question on the biggest porch in North America at the Grand Hotel on Mackinac Island. We didn't know it then, but it was the same hotel my father was sent to after the war to recover. Of course, I said "Yes!"

Dennis would become my husband and Dad would walk me down the aisle, taking his role as my real father to a very special level. For all the things he had missed in my life, this would be one big moment we could still have together.

Dennis surprised me with an engagement party at his brownstone.

Everyone held champagne flutes and yelled, "Surprise!" as we walked in the door. I was stunned to see Mom standing next to my future mother-in-law, Marilyn. How'd she get here? When did all this planning happen? Den, ever the planner/instigator, had flown Mom in from Ohio so she wouldn't miss a thing,

"I can't believe you flew in my mother!" I said hugging Dennis, who truly had thought of everything.

There were more hugs and hellos when Dad and Soozie arrived, and I nearly fell over watching Soozie and Mom chatting like schools girls. It struck me how similar they were. Creative and artsy, they were beauties who bubbled over with effervescence.

It was there that I realized my father needed the kind of woman who lived from her emotions, since it was hard for him to tap into his. I knew he'd loved his mother for her warmth and kindness, which was so unlike his father, who he thought of as cold and judgmental. It made sense that he would seek out the same kind of woman—and I think it's also why he felt so at ease with me. We all bubbled, which allowed him to make like a sponge and soak it up.

Dad was more than happy that we wanted to get married in Newport, and dug right in to help with the planning and paying for the wedding.

That had been the easy part. Finding a date proved to be a lot harder because we needed to find a time that wouldn't conflict with TV ratings. We settled on August 1st, 2003 at Saint Augustin's Church in Newport, followed by a black tie reception at the famous Rosecliff Mansion. Dad was pleased with the plans and excited to start creating a guest list. It would be his big day, too.

As the day drew closer, I grew giddy with excitement whenever I envisioned Dad walking down the aisle and giving me away to join Dennis. My Aunt Kathy had found the perfect song for our father-daughter dance—"I believe in Happy Endings" by Neil Diamond. I cried the first time I heard the lyrics:

I believe in extra innings, starry skies and dreams come true,

I believed it since I first met you...

I believe in extra innings brand new starts and hearts that care the way I do...

That song still makes me cry today every time I play it.

I was counting down the days until my fairytale wedding when I got a chilling call from Soozie. "Kara, honey, your dad is in the hospital, there's something wrong with his stomach."

I held my breath. "Is it serious?"

"They don't know. He went to the emergency room, He's in a lot of pain. I'll call you when I know more." She sounded as though she'd been crying, and my heart went out to her because my own heart was heavy worrying about Dad.

Soozie called back later to say that tests revealed a blockage in my father's digestive system. I dropped everything and told my bosses I needed to go to Rhode Island immediately.

At first it seemed like this would work itself out, and I returned to work hoping to hear good news. But as days went on, he grew weaker and sicker, so I made another trip to the hospital to see him. He was dropping weight rapidly and I was shocked to see how quickly he'd become a shadow of his former self.

"Hi, Dad, how are you feeling?" I asked, choking back tears.

"Terrible, just awful. I have never been this sick in my entire life." Spent, he rolled over to go back to sleep.

I had never seen him like this, and was absolutely terrified as I drove back home. My father was such a force of nature that it was impossible to ever picture him sick.

When I returned to the hospital on my day off, he looked weak and ashen. After hugging him, I immediately went to the bathroom in his room, shut the door, and collapsed on the floor sobbing. How could this happen? Is he going to miss my wedding? Then the fear really kicked in: Is he going to die?

As much as I loved Dennis, I couldn't bear the thought of not having my dad at our wedding.

I took some deep breaths, wiped my tears and went back to his bedside, where I held his hand. He looked up at me with soft eyes. "I'm really sick, Kara. Always make sure you keep an eye on your stomach, it's my weak spot, and it may be yours, too. The nurses want to pump my stomach, but I wouldn't let them."

I blinked. "What do you mean you won't let them?"

"I can't stand the thought of having something down my throat. I won't do it."

I couldn't believe what I was hearing. He needed to get better. I needed him so much! "Dad, you'll only feel it for a second when it goes in. After that, you'll start to feel so much better."

He looked almost hopeful. "Are you sure I'll only feel it going in?"

"Yes." I nodded to punctuate the point.

"Ok then, I'll do it." Always so headstrong, I could have danced around the room after he agreed, reluctantly, to listen to me. I left while they did the procedure. He started to feel better almost instantly, and the color came back to his face. *Thank God*. It looked like Dad would be able to make it to the wedding, though doctors cautioned that he had a long way to go. It was harder to bounce back and at the age of eighty-three.

Unfortunately, resting wasn't one of my father's skills, so each time I came to the hospital, he had more on his To Do list, and as bizarre as this sounds his number one priority was making sure Dennis and the groomsmen gave up on the idea of wearing plaid pants to the rehearsal dinner.

"Patterned trousers?" he grimaced. "That's just awful, awful." He got so flustered, he needed water.

Here the man was fighting to get better, and all he could think about was what people were going to wear to the rehearsal dinner? I could have laughed if he wasn't so genuinely upset about it. "Dad, Dennis loves the preppy madras and wale pants, and the *only* thing he cared about was wearing crazy pants with his groomsmen to the rehearsal dinner." I privately wondered if the drugs were making him crazy. Why on earth does he care?

"It's dreadful, Kara!" he said with as much strength as he could muster. "They can wear khakis or Nantucket Reds, but no patterned trousers!"

Dennis gave in, figuring he couldn't deny a man's near-death-bed-wish, and my father called up a store on Nantucket and overnighted Dennis some new pants. At least they could be colored!

I knew his juice was coming back when he started calling the stationery shop to have the wedding invitations sent by courier to anyone who stopped by to visit him in the hospital. The list kept growing, and I worried we were going to exceed the maximum number of 240 people allowed inside Rosecliff. But Dad didn't seem to care, saying to the doctors and nurses who were caring for him, "If you get me well enough to go to my daughter's wedding, you are all invited."

Thankfully, they didn't hold him to that, or we might have had to get a tent for all the extras. But they worked hard to get Dad well, and released him the night before my rehearsal dinner. He was weak and frail, having lost thirty pounds, but he was out and determined to walk me down the aisle. I was thanking God every second, hoping he wouldn't relapse.

Worried looks passed over the faces of those at the rehearsal dinner when they caught sight of his frail appearance. He'd made it, but he was unable to talk or stand for very long, and left early. But dad was still a fighter, and he showed up a new man the next day at the church. Seeing him, I walked as fast as my wedding dress would allow so I could give him a tight hug. "Thank God you made it!" I wasn't afraid of walking down the aisle, but the thought of having to do it without him was paralyzing.

"Hey, baby, you look beautiful," Dad said, smiling as he saw me in my dress for the first time. "That is one of the most beautiful wedding gowns I've ever seen."

"Thanks, Dad, but what about you? How do you feel?" I was secretly mortified at how his tuxedo hung on him.

"I'm fine," he replied, in his customary strong voice. "I'm back to the weight I was in high school, and I'm going to keep it that way!"

We laughed, and I smoothed down a few of his wiry stray hairs. While we waited for our cue to walk, *The New York Times* photographer snapped away for the vows article that would be in the Sunday Style section.

When the music cued up, Dad grabbed my hand with his strong forceful grip, and I knew he was going to be okay. The excitement seemed to energize him, and we walked hand in hand, smiling ear to ear as flashbulbs clicked. Cameras from the local Rhode Island stations, as well as one from my own station, were there, plus a few newspaper photographers. I couldn't help but think how much sweeter this was than our infamous news conference ten years ago. It was the happily-ever-after picture I'd dreamed of.

Ten years of forgiving, laughing, loving, testing, and just figuring it all out, had created a real father-daughter relationship—a relationship we treasured and counted on. We walked down the aisle, aware of the importance of this day—our loved ones tearing up with joy, and the press looking at us to witness what we had become.

I had waited a lifetime to meet both of these important men in my life, and my wedding day made my love official for both of them. As we approached the altar I kissed my father's cheek and took Dennis' hand.

At the reception, I worried my father might lose steam and not be able to hold out for his speech and our father-daughter dance, but every time I looked at him, he was talking and smiling as if nothing was wrong. His sheer will to be there seemed to transcend his exhaustion.

Cameras clicked as Dad and I danced to Neil Diamond's "Happy Endings."

My father was a fabulous dancer and I just tried to keep up with him as he spun me around the floor. It was an exhilarating fairytale moment. We both beamed as we made box steps across the mansion floor, while news cameras clicked away. For the thousandth time since my first summer with Dad, I thought about how we were no longer performing—we had overcome many awkward steps, and had found our rhythm. I wasn't the "love child" from newspaper headlines anymore—I was his daughter, period. That steady drumbeat of my inner voice that had told me to have faith all those years ago had finally won out and gave way to a new heartsong—not just for me, but for both of us.

When the song ended, he flashed me a look of "uh oh— need a chair. Now." Dad rested while Dennis danced with my mother to "My Girl," one of Mom's favorites. All the years of discord, anger, hurt, and jealousy, it was wonderful to see the beaming smile spread across her face. With all she'd been through, she deserved it. Despite our differences, she'd stepped aside and allowed me to find my way with my father, no matter how much it hurt, and I was happy she was getting recognition for her selflessness.

When it came time for my father to take the microphone, I'd hoped, prayed actually, that he might say something that would help bring closure for Mom, but I didn't expect his words to be so directed at her:

"I'm so happy Kara has found as great a man as she has in Dennis. I couldn't be more proud of these two young people. They are both Emmy Award winning journalists at the number one station in Hartford, which by the way, all you Rhode Islanders here should know that is a much bigger market than Providence…" the whole room erupted in laughter , then came one of Dad's famous long pauses…"I don't deserve any credit for those things—the credit goes to Kara's mother, Judy Vargo, who raised her alone, teaching her all of the important things in life, a love for God, country and family…."

I felt the sting of tears, and Dennis squeezed my hand. My father was finally saying all the things I'd wished he'd say—and he was saying it in front of the most important people in our lives. It was the first time he had ever acknowledged all that my mother had done, and even expressed gratitude for it. The guests clapped like crazy, and Mom's face had a renewed glow as Dad finished his remarks. I stood up to hug my father, "Thank you so much, Dad..." I whispered. "...for everything — and especially for what you just did for Mom. I love you." I gave him a big kiss.

"Love you, too — but I need to sit down," he said, pointing toward his chair.

He had rallied for his mission, but now that it was complete, he was fading fast. I helped him back to his chair as Mom moved toward him.

"Bruce, that was such a great speech. Thank you. Aren't you happy that we ended up with this amazing daughter?"

"Yes, I am," he said smiling.

Before he could say anything more, Soozie and Marjorie walked over to give my Mom a hug, "Congratulations, Judy!"

Suddenly, my father was surrounded by three women whose lives had orbited his over the years. They all gathered around his chair and planted kisses on him in unison. The photographer snapped away while Dad scrunched up his face like he was being attacked.

That picture pretty much says it all — they'd loved him in spite of his flaws. It was all so bizarre, I still can't quite wrap my head around it. The picture is hysterical, and I keep it framed in my family room today.

After the photo, Dad started to fade; it was about all he could take, and he needed to leave.

"It's a wonderful party, Kara, and I hate to leave — but I need to go home and rest. I'll see you tomorrow."

"It's okay, Dad. I'm just grateful you made it. I love you."

I gave Dad and Soozie one last big hug and kiss and headed back to the dance floor.

My father had used every ounce of strength he had to be at my wedding, and now it was time for him to bail out. He did his job well. *The New York Times* reported, "Remember those two from ten years ago? They really are father and daughter now."

Soon after the wedding Dennis and I decided we wanted to sell his condo in Newport and buy a vacation house together so we could begin building more memories in the town that gave me my father and my husband. I joked about wanting to move back to my father's street, Cliff Avenue, where the journey began, and Dennis mentioned he knew a house was for sale there, and it was on the affordable side of the street before the private end where my father's estate had been. We made an appointment and decided to buy the house after only ten minutes inside. I have spent longer picking out a sweater, but this felt so right. Our little three bedroom cape style abode would be a place to create a new family life with all the love that had grown from this special spot.

18 Dad Becomes Poppy

I knew children were the next step in my life, but I was worried that my unusual upbringing would leave me ill-equipped to be the mother I wanted to be. I still thought of my friends' lives as the gold standard and thought I might need to do some more healing before I could be the great mom and wife I wanted to be, so I decided to go to therapy.

Aimee Golbert, a therapist in West Hartford, had a calm voice and razor sharp intuition, which I needed since I found it difficult to access my feelings sometimes. Like my father, talking about my feelings didn't always come naturally. My ability to detach from my emotions in times of crisis made them hard to retrieve, and even harder to talk about. I reasoned there could be some cracks from growing up fatherless and helping Mom battle some tough times, and I wasn't sure how they were affecting me. My new life appeared perfect from the outside, and I needed to feel assured it was equally perfect on the inside. I wanted to learn more about who I was and heal anything still buried down below, so Aimee had me use a sand tray to help *show* my inner state.

She asked me to choose several small objects and figurines from the shelves in her sunny office and place them in what looked like a small sandbox. When I was done she asked me to tell her what each represented. I had chosen an egg, because it was hard on the outside and jiggly in the middle, which is how I often felt. I also chose a rubbery skeleton that looked ill and put it at the bottom of the tray. To me, it represented how deep down I felt like a part of me was damaged. Even though my father had entered my life and his love for me was genuine, there were old parts of me that were scarred and resistant to heal—those were the parts that still erupted in anger when I felt overwhelmed, or when things got too chaotic. Aimee explained that my goal was to be aware of my feelings so I could understand how those parts of me affected my adult life.

Though I had forgiven my father, my old fear of rejection and abandonment was still imprinted on my soul. Living in an unstable environment with Mom had only compounded the problem. But I'd learned I didn't have to live with my old wiring—I'd already proven my ability to upgrade my system when my father entered my life. But I needed to be aware of unhealed wounds before I could release the old patterns that no longer served me, and create new pathways to peace. My huge "ah ha" moment came when I realized that it's never too late to heal, and finding my father— regardless of my age—was transformational. My bruises didn't have to define me. My parents were flawed, like we all are, and now it was my job to heal myself and pave a better way for the next generation. My bruises had made me strong and, once I learned how to love them, I felt better about setting out to love a child. I started to see my tough lessons as gifts that made me a survivor, instead of as defects that made me less than whole.

While on my journey to self-discovery, one of my favorite books had been *Sacred Contracts* by Caroline Myss. She wrote about how our soul makes a contract to learn certain lessons on earth, and the biggest relationships in our lives play out to help us heal and grow. This was cathartic for me because I believed that my father and I cosmically agreed to take this journey, through the fields of hurt and mountains of joy, so our souls could come out stronger. Myss says orphaned spirits are often leaders, which really resonated with me. Regardless, I am grateful for the strength of the journey. Maybe I'll never know why it had to be the way it was, but I trust in the perfection of the lessons.

My father loved to say life is all about just the facts: "Who, what, where, when, and how—the why doesn't matter." The "why" has *always* mattered to me, but I've learned it will only be revealed when the timing is right. Until then, it's faith that has to lead. My faith helped me follow our sacred path to wholeness, and I have learned to surrender to my still, small voice that always knows the *why*.

Aimee liked to compare my psyche to a house. The window dressing was what I showed the world, and the basement was where I was digging for answers. I wanted to open up my old boxes to see what was in there and do some housecleaning before I brought anyone new home. I wanted to take my time, and make sure I built a solid foundation for my children, since I didn't want my little ones to feel wobbly like I did.

Of course, it didn't take long after we got back from our honeymoon from Italy for our parents to start asking about babies. Mom had moved into my old condo that was across the street from our Hartford brownstone, where we would start our new life. She had hopes of being close to us and any future grandchildren. Dennis and I wanted kids, but I was still building my career and working weekends, so I wasn't sure how being a mom would fit in right away. I was only twenty-eight, so my biological clock wasn't ticking. But Dad's clock was. He was now eighty-three years old, and I was worried if we didn't start a family soon, he might not be around to become a grandfather to my kids. We waited a year before trying to start a family.

Dennis was beyond excited to become a father. We couldn't wait to tell our parents I was pregnant, but we wanted to do it in person. Unfortunately, before we could even get anyone together to share the happy news, I started cramping, feeling very sick, and bleeding. I called in sick to work and spent the day crumpled up in a ball in our bed crying. Dennis looked helpless as I spoke to the doctor on the phone, waiting for the official word he'd feared.

"They say I'm probably having a miscarriage," I said, choking back a sob as I hung up the phone. "Since I'm only six weeks along, there's nothing to do but let it pass."

"I'm so sorry," he said, hugging me as we both cried.

My innocence of being a happy new mom had dissolved. Even though doctors told us miscarriage was common, it didn't make it hurt any less.

Instead of sharing happy news, we called our parents to let them know I'd suffered a miscarriage. Dad felt awful and started calling me every day to ask how I was doing. Since we decided not to tell anyone at work, I looked forward to my phone ringing during the day, knowing Dad could bring a smile to my face, even if the conversations were always brief,

"Hi, just calling to touch your base." This was Dad's unique phrase for checking in. I felt his constant care through his daily calls and quick voicemail messages asking "Can I do anything?" His little pokes of love helped me heal, and I was even more excited for a baby to arrive someday.

Someday seemed to be taking too long, and I went to see my obstetrician, Stephen Fishman, M.D., for a consultation. He told me the silver lining was I had gotten pregnant before, but since we had been trying for more than a year, I was now classified as infertile, even though all the testing showed we were normal. I feared that deep down my broken childhood was preventing me from becoming a mom. What if something deep down in my basement was blocking a baby? Could old fears prevent me from giving into motherhood? I told my doctor I would see a specialist, but that I also wanted "something else." I didn't know what that was, but I knew a deeper part of me was asking to explore the meaning behind these disappointments. My soul wanted to know the "Why?" Dr. Fishman referred me to his wife, Doreen Fishman, a holistic nurse, who was also an energy healer.

I had no idea what to expect when I arrived for my appointment. Doreen guided me to a massage table that was covered in a blanket of silken jewel tone patches with a round pillow to support my knees or lower back. I lay down and tried to just relax.

"Are you comfortable?" She asked as she laid the soft blanket on top of me.

This was all so new to me, and I felt a bit awkward.

"Just relax while I guide you through a meditation."

Doreen's soothing voice brought me to a beach where sunlight poured in through the top of my head, what she called my crown chakra. She asked me to focus on the center of my chest and imagine a white pilot light expanding throughout my heart and filling every cell in my body. As Doreen laid her hands gently on my feet, I slipped into a void of utter peace. It seemed like I fell asleep, but when I came to, she said I had done great work.

"What do you mean? I don't think I did anything."

She brought me to her couch and poured me a cup of herbal tea. "What did you experience?"

My mind flashed on a scene of angels at a brook of bubbling water on a beautiful sunny day. They gently washed my back and told me, "We have been waiting for you to wake up."

As I told her the story, I didn't for one second consider my "dream" to be a real place. "I'm not sure what that means, but it felt very peaceful." I hoped she would enlighten me to any hidden meanings.

"Yes, that is what they wanted you to feel. I don't get the feeling you have any medical problems, but you do have a lot of anxiety, and that can prevent women from conceiving. Emotions can and do affect our physical bodies in very concrete ways, Kara. Just relax and surrender to the journey of being a mother. I feel an energy around you, and I think your dream of being a mother will happen soon, when the divine timing is right."

"An energy around me? You mean a soul?" My rational brain had a hard time grasping all this, but on a deeper level—a level I didn't know existed—everything she'd said felt right.

According to Doreen, we all have a spiritual support team who is always trying to guide us to the lessons our souls need to learn on earth. It was a lot to take in. Angels? Unborn spirits? As strange as it all sounded, I left her home with a strong sense that I would get pregnant. That same voice that told me to find Dad was telling me I would have a baby, but I needed to surrender to the waiting. I couldn't script having a baby any more than I could script the happy ending with my father. Once again, I was learning to just have faith, even when the answers didn't make any sense.

I was never the same after leaving Doreen's office, and I started to realize my quest to have a baby was a spiritual journey, just as all the big things in my life had been...especially finding Dad. I wanted to know more about the world on the other side of the veil that Doreen could so easily access. If everything that happened in my life was part of my soul's contract, then I wanted to better understand the terms.

I left feeling happier and lighter than I had in a long time, and it was only a few months later that I got pregnant. This time, I had a good feeling it would stick. I was more relaxed and sensed I'd learned a valuable lesson about surrendering—something my soul wanted me to understand.

We announced the pregnancy to our parents telling them they couldn't say anything to anyone until I was at least twelve weeks along. Later, our mothers treasured the first ultrasound pictures of their first grandchild, looking at them with oohs and aahs, already dreaming of the baby shopping trips.

Not surprisingly, Dad couldn't figure out what the little black and white blob was supposed to show him, and was surprised at our decision to be surprised about the gender of the baby. "Can't they tell you if it's a boy of girl nowadays?"

I nodded. "Yes, but we want to wait. It's one of the last big surprises left in life."

"I don't understand how two reporters don't want to find out crucial information. That's just crazy. Who, what, where, when, and how is all that matters. The why is subjective and irrelevant."

"Um, Dad, we know *why* I'm pregnant," I said, teasing. Bless him for only dealing in facts. Some things would always elude him. "You'll have to wait for the other information."

Mom, on the other hand, loved to speculate and kept telling me her vibes told her it would be a boy with blonde curly hair. "You know your Mom is psychic. I was right about Dennis, remember that?"

"Yes, Mom." That was hard to refute.

"If it's a boy, are you going to name him Bruce?" I could tell she wasn't crazy about the idea.

"We're not sharing any names, so you'll have to wait until the baby arrives." The last thing I needed were more opinions from our overly opinionated family.

She needn't have worried. Dad told me he didn't like his name anyway. However, he did have to get in on the act, and promptly mailed us a copy of *Town and Country Baby Names*. I think it was his way of ensuring we would choose a name that was "appropriate" according to Newport standards, and not follow the latest Hollywood trend of naming babies after fruit.

And he didn't stop at names. He wanted to buy something for the baby, and I suggested a baby blanket he or she would always have. In typical Dad fashion—because he never did anything halfway—he took me to an exclusive trunk show for fancy French linens by Leron, hosted at an oceanfront home in Newport, and ordered a white pique baby blanket monogrammed with an aqua gingham "H" for House. It was obvious Dad wanted to continue his tradition of monogramming everything. The custom-made heirloom was so nice I was scared to use it, fearing it would easily be ruined. Instead, I decided to drape it over the crib in our nursery as a decoration. I wanted to preserve it so one day I could tell my children this was a gift from Poppy.

With everything going on, I made time to go back and see Doreen. I was excited to tune into what my soul had to say about the soul that was coming soon.

"I can tell you the baby feels very wanted."

"You mean you can tell I want the baby?" I asked.

"That too—but this soul told me it feels very loved."

She said she saw beautiful, luminescent light from the angels all around me and the baby.

"Hmmm—um...wow." I was unsure of what to make of this.

I was aware the little soul I was carrying had the power to transform us as a family. They say raising children gives us an opportunity to heal old wounds, and I sensed my own soul was trying to make me aware of this divine opportunity. A baby was a new beginning that allowed Dad to become Poppy, and heal me all over again by giving the baby the love I missed out on in my early years. It was also a chance for Mom and Dad to become grandparents, instead of just ex-lovers.

As the baby grew inside of me, so did my spiritual curiosity. I started to make time for silence each day so I could feel my own inner guidance more. At first I was demanding. I wanted to touch it, talk to it, ask it how it spoke to me, give it a megaphone and ask it to talk louder. Being a reporter means I'm nosy and impatient, so it's natural I wanted answers. Yesterday. I thought if these mysterious universal forces helped me find Dad and now have a baby, I wanted to know how they work.

Okay, soul, just talk to me and make it quick, I have stuff to do.

Doreen taught me that Truth moves at a slower frequency, and it starts with tuning into yourself and slowing down—not something I wanted to hear but earnestly gave it a try. Even today, it's still hard for me to slow down, but I know that silence is a requirement to have peace. Ever the restless reporter, I've tried to ask my inner voice to speak up and talk louder, only to remember that it's my job to quiet down. One of the reasons I do stories on mindfulness and healing is because we tend to teach that which we need to learn. I'm happy to say that after eight years of reporting *Kara's Cures* for the mind, body, and spirit, I have mastered a bit more patience.

The day I went into labor, we were anything but patient. Dennis called our parents right away so they could race to the hospital, only to wait, and wait some more. While I was pushing, Dennis tried to keep tabs on our parents by checking in from time to time. Since the baby was taking its sweet time of making an appearance, I worried about any fireworks that might happen with my parents locked in a waiting room together for hours. At least Soozie was there, too, and she was a calming presence for Dad. And thankfully, she and Mom got along great. Plus cousin Fenton was there, which always meant we'd be assured of some comic relief. He had never witnessed a baby being born and couldn't wait to be part of the action.

"What's it look like out there?" I asked Dennis in between sucking on ice chips.

"Your father arrived with two giant stuffed bears, one pink and one blue. He says he wants to be prepared."

I couldn't help but laugh over my contraction.

After a long and exhausting labor I gave birth to a baby girl on February 23rd, 2007. Dennis cut her cord and placed her swaddled, warm body on my chest. We fell instantly in love, and I was transformed by a feeling of exuberance I'd never experienced before. She was perfect. She had a ton of thick jet black hair and olive skin, and clearly favored Dennis's Italian side.

After the nurses gave the go-ahead for visitors, Dennis grabbed the video camera and raced outside to tell our parents the news. His plan was to videotape their reactions so I could watch them later, which frustrated our eager parents to no end, since they had to wait for Dennis to set up the camera before he finally said, "It's a girl!"

My father grabbed the pink bear and leaped to his feet, moving much faster than most eight-seven-year-olds, and looked like he was ready to break the door down to see the baby and me. My mother was giddy and jumping around like a cheerleader, while Dennis's mom started crying, thrilled to finally have a girl since she only had boys in her family.

Of course they all wanted to know the name, but Dennis kept the suspense going. "Kara wants to be the one to tell you her name."

My creators entered the delivery room. As they jockeyed for a space close to me and the baby, I realized the little bundle of joy in my arms, our little girl, had the power to bring my parents together in love. She would only know them as her grandparents and not the warring souls they had been for me.

"Her name is Helena Sundlun House," I announced.

"It means beautiful," Dennis said—and she was clearly that.

Dad's eyes lit up when he heard we had chosen Sundlun. I knew it might upset Mom, but I didn't know how much longer I would have Dad, and I wanted him to share in our joy and see how we'd honored his name. I promised Mom the next baby would have a name from our mothers' sides.

Everyone took turns holding Helena, starting with Mom and Dennis' mother, Marilyn. When it was my father's turn, he seemed nervous since babies weren't exactly his forté. He sat down in a chair, and we carefully placed Helena in his lap. Holding her tightly, his tough exterior melted as he gazed into her tiny face. Her birth was the game changer that made everyone want to do better, love more, and heal the past.

Fenton's words summed it up best when he got his turn, "Amazing! I mean really amazing! This is just incredible—so cool!"

In the weeks to come, our mothers jumped in with offers to bring food, offer advice, and volunteer to babysit so Dennis and I could sleep. Dad called every evening. Sometimes I was nursing the baby and could only listen to him talk on the answering machine: "Kara, it's Dad. Just want you to know I'm thinking of you and wanted to know how that beautiful baby, Helena, is doing. Call me back. Love you."

Having a baby opened up a new avenue for Dad to show his love, a path to show his soft side in a way that didn't scare him. He could do things for Helena he missed out on with me, like buying her presents, coming to her christening, and playing with her in the sand at his home in Jamaica for Christmas vacation.

Occasionally, he still needed to be reminded about how to be a Grade-A Poppy. As Helena's first birthday approached, we were busy planning a big party at our home for the family. Dad and Soozie planned to drive down, until duty called. Hillary Clinton was running for President and wanted my father at her fundraiser in Rhode Island.

"Kara, I have to go—I'm the last sitting Democratic governor in the state. The party needs me there, and I want Hillary to win in Rhode Island."

"Really—well, I want you at Helena's birthday party," I shot back. I was upset he couldn't see which one was more important. Sure, he could have seen her another day, but I wanted pictures of Poppy holding Helena on her first birthday. I wanted to rack up the moments, since we had missed way too many—and I thought he owed me this. I decided I wasn't going to make this easy on him. He should be there, and that was that.

After about a week, Dad came up with a solution. He was going to attend Clinton's fundraiser, then get his friend, who owned a private plane, to take him to Hartford in time to cut the cake.

"I might be a little late, but I'll be there."

Dad made it, and enjoyed watching Helena bop to the children's musician we had brought in. Later, she crawled up on his lap to grab his nose, one of her favorite things to do, as we tried to teach her to say, "Poppy, Poppy."

"Pa, Pa," she mimicked.

Dad had figured out a way to make it right, and I couldn't help but laugh that we had a great story for Helena's baby book. Dad had always been a man of extremes and would stop at nothing to get something done, so this was his way of getting the job done. In the grand scheme of things, Helena wouldn't have known or cared whether Dad was there or not, but *I* needed him there. Showing up to her parties went a long way to helping me forgive him for missing all of mine. Sometimes I still had to teach him what was important, but I loved him for being willing to learn.

Having Mom at the party was equally important, and I never got tired of watching her bouncing Helena around. "Your Gigi loves you, yes, she does. You're my little baby."

All that love pouring out of Mom made her more at ease around my father, and that made it easier on me. I didn't have to worry about her getting upset over Dad as much, since she was so focused on the baby. Evolution was underway!

If planning Helena's birthday party—and convincing Dad we were more important than Hillary—wasn't enough, I discovered the morning of the party that I was pregnant. After all my struggles the first time around, I was shocked and relieved. The timing could have been better, since this was the morning of a big party and I had to focus on that. But what a miracle! It happened without even trying.

The memories of my miscarriage had taught Dennis and me to be more cautious, so we decided we would break the news a couple months later at Easter, when the whole family would be together.

Dennis's brother, Chris, and his lovely wife, Jodi, had offered to host an Easter egg hunt for the kids at their new home in Walpole, Massachusetts. Their son, Tommy, was born nine weeks before Helena, and I loved the fact she'd have a cousin her age to hunt for those eggs. Dennis, always the producer, came up with the idea of stuffing our ultrasound pics into plastic Easter eggs and giving one to each family member to open. Our mothers, along with my father and Soozie, would all be there, so it seemed like the perfect plan.

As Helena and her cousin, Tommy, played on the floor, Dennis passed out the plastic eggs to each family member. "Kara and I have a special Easter gift for you all."

My sister in-law Jodi figured it out first. "Oh my God! Congratulations, they're having a baby!"

The moms and Soozie got it seconds later, but my dad seemed a little confused.

"Honey, that's an ultrasound picture of the baby they are going to have," Soozie explained.

"Well, that's wonderful," he said, turning the paper around to find the baby. "Doesn't look like much now, though."

"Dad, the white outline there is the baby," I said, laughing.

Moments later, Tommy came into the living room wearing a t-shirt that said, "I'm going to be a big brother" on the front.

"Oh my gosh! Congrats to you, too!" I said, hugging Jodi. "Can you believe it, babies at the same time again? That's awesome!"

"We're due November 6th," I said

"That's my due date, too!" Jodi shouted excitedly.

The synchronicities of our lives were almost unbelievable. We had both gotten married in Newport, and now we were having babies at the exact same time, creating a bevy of cousins to make family events fun. It all seemed so meant to be, until it wasn't.

19 Who Do You Want In the Foxhole?

At nineteen weeks, I lost the baby. In a cruel quirk of fate, my doctor informed me the baby hadn't formed correctly and my pregnancy was not viable. Once again, the sting of miscarriage burned through our hearts, only this time it hurt even more. We thought we had made it into the safety zone only to have to face losing a baby we already loved so much. Unlike last time, everyone, even the TV viewers, knew I was pregnant.

Mom called non-stop, trying to get answers from Dennis that we just didn't have. "Kara, this is your mother, please call me right away. I really need to know what's going on."

When I didn't call back right away, she called again, and again.

Each time I saw "Mom calling" across my cell phone, I knew she was trying to understand it all so she could be there for me during this horrible time. But I didn't want to talk to anyone. I just lay motionless in bed, popping Advil on schedule. I couldn't bring myself to talk yet, I lacked the energy to try and explain the unexplainable, so I just let Dennis field the calls from family.

My father had left a long message on Dennis's cell phone. "I just want you to know I'm here for you. I am so sorry. I can't imagine what you both must feel, but I'm here, I'll do anything for you. I don't want to intrude, but Soozie and I are here if you need us. Love you."

When I finally got the strength to call him back, the tears welled up in me the minute he said hello. My emotional walls were collapsing, and I couldn't say anything. I needed him to be my rock, someone to crash into besides Dennis, who needed to do his own grieving.

Dad was always so proud of his ability to take a mess and fix it. From broken companies to shattered economies, Dad was the guy you called when you had to clean up a mess. He couldn't fix this for me, but his instincts to stand back and listen were exactly what I needed. His strong, reassuring voice repeated offers to help, but he didn't badger me with what I needed him to do. His nightly calls were like a buoy in my sea of pain.

"How are we today?" he would ask.

If I didn't get my phone right away, he would keep calling, trying to find me to make sure I hadn't slipped too far into a depression. "Kara, it's Dad, hoping you're okay. Call me soon."

Though my father didn't raise me, somehow his instincts told him exactly the right way to care for me. My own emotions were so fried, and I needed someone cool and calm around me. Conversely, my mother's heart was breaking for me, and her own distressed emotional state was too much for me to face. She absorbed and amplified my pain, while Dad managed it.

With my family's support, I eventually pulled back into the realm of doing okay, but I still wanted to know *why* this happened to me. My spiritual core centered on my belief that everything happens for a reason, even if I don't understand the divine timing. It was a belief that helped me on my quest to find my father, to marry my husband, and have my daughter. I remembered the spiritual messages on Doreen's table when I was pregnant with Helena, and wondered what the angels could be telling me now. I wanted a sign. *Dear God, just give me a sign.*

I looked out the window and saw a coyote in my driveway. I was still on painkillers and wondered if I was delirious since we lived in a busy city next to a main road where coyotes were not part of the landscape.

"Dennis, come here! Is that a coyote?" I asked.

"Oh wow…yeah, I think it is," he said, rushing to grab his camera.

He snapped shots of the wild beast on our blacktop and sent them into the station to use them on the news—a coyote in the city was a good talker. While Dennis captured this strange sight, something told me there was a deeper meaning than my eyes could see. Then my inner voice tried to speak. Something told me to Google "spiritual meaning of coyote." A website reported that the coyote is associated with a "deep magic of life and creation," saying if a coyote crosses your path there is "hidden wisdom for you to reap…Call on the coyote to support you in refreshing your perspective, and lighten the weight of your circumstances."

Could the coyote in my driveway be a sign telling me to have faith? Once again, it all sounded crazy, but the deeper place inside me felt a sense of peace wash over me, and I just knew everything would be okay, even though my heart was still breaking.

I had toughened up my spiritual muscle on my journey to find Dad, and once again, my faith was being tested. But this time, I knew more about surrender. Of course, my arms ached to hold my baby, and I cried puddles of tears because I'm human and I hurt. While faith doesn't take away the pain, it takes away the fear. If my experience of finding Dad taught me anything, it was about trusting in the process without fear. And now I didn't have to go it alone. I'd found Dad, and he was right there waiting to shield me if I couldn't take the flak. Just knowing that made me feel safer and better able to weather the battle ahead.

Dad loved to say, "You know who you want in your foxhole when you see how they act under pressure."

My father was someone I wanted in my foxhole—he knew exactly how to protect me without making me feel like I would suffocate. He also helped me with damage control: "Kara, what will the station do without you, and how will they handle this story?"

"They'll have to make an announcement on my show, and on the news, since everyone knew I was pregnant. My bosses are being great and have told me to take all the time I need, I don't know when I'm going back yet."

"Make sure you rest and take all the time you need. I know you, so don't try to rush it."

He knew me, because I was like him. Funny, I was getting a lesson in patience from a man who had none. At the age of eighty-eight, he still went to the office every morning because he thought he had to.

"Thanks, Dad, I won't." I felt better about missing work after my hard-driving father just told me to stay on the couch. He had been a media mogul and knew how competitive my field was. Usually, he would have advised me to work harder, get there first, go home last, but instead, he was urging me to slow down and just take care of myself. It was exactly what I needed to hear in order to let go of any guilt and angst about taking a leave of absence from my job.

I still had to worry about the fact that our very private pain would need a public explanation. I had long passed the three month quiet period, and we hadn't worried about sharing my adventures in pregnancy with the audience. Handmade blankets and booties from viewers piled up on my desk.

Now, my co-host on *Better Connecticut*, Scot Haney—who's better known for his zany antics—had to make a very serious announcement: "Kara and Dennis have suffered a miscarriage. Our thoughts and prayers are with them during this difficult time."

Dennis's co-anchor, Denise D'Ascenzo, who was like a big sister to me, appeared close to tears when she made a similar announcement on the evening news before calling to comfort me.

"I know how painful this is, Kara, and my heart is breaking for you both. If I can give you any advice, it's to just take your time— it'll be a long time before you feel like yourself again. I'm praying for you."

Denise had been such a role model for me—she had been the face of our station for more than twenty years, and was the epitome of professionalism and grace under fire. She confided she'd been through the exact same thing, and knew how hard it was to come back to work. She also told me to listen to my father: "He's right, Kara. Your father is a wise man, so listen to him and take all the time you need. Your career will be there when you're better."

Dad didn't consider himself a spiritual man, and he wouldn't have shared my excitement about the coyote "sign," but I think he was trying to teach me what he wished he would have learned earlier. He knew we were both wired for charging forward, but he wanted me to know it was also okay to take a step back—that he would still love me, even if I was wallowing on the couch instead of winning Emmys.

Sympathy cards replaced baby gifts at the station, and I wanted to crawl in a hole and hide. I appreciated the love, but I wasn't ready to mourn in public. I decided to just listen to my father and crawl up with popsicles and cry when I felt like it. Mostly, I focused on Helena, our beautiful girl who could always make me smile.

Dad was right to tell me not to worry about work, but it helped when our General Manager, Klarn DePalma, called to tell Dennis he was thinking of us and offered to help in any way we needed. Dana Neves, our News Director who had the same due date as I did, and Patience Hettrick, our assistant News Director, were both young mothers, and brought a box of yummy baked goods to my house.

"We know you love your chocolate," they said, enveloping me in a warm hug. In spite of my sadness, I was so grateful for our co-workers at Channel Three—they were a second family, and they grieved right along with us.

When I finally did return to work, the head of Meredith Broadcasting, Paul Karpowicz, came into the studio as I was getting mic'd up for my first live *Better Connecticut*. He didn't ask me anything and, instead, just gave me a big hug. "We're so happy to have you back."

I was stunned the man in charge of all fourteen of our TV stations made time in his busy day to offer me some support, and it gave me the courage I needed to start the show. Paul had also been a Rhode Islander and knew my father, and I think he felt like giving me a little paternal support at a time when I needed it.

The opening music rolled, the audience clapped more loudly than usual, and my smile turned on. Getting back to doing the job I loved turned out to be great medicine. I left work knowing I could find the old me—it would just take a little time. I was happy to know my father would be in the foxhole for as long as it took.

20 Born Again: Old Souls, New Baby

Life started again, I was getting back into my groove of taping shows, anchoring the news, and setting up interviews for my series *Kara's Cures*, which focuses on ways to better the mind, body, and spirit. The Hartford Family Institute was holding a forum on grief and wanted me to interview Kerrie O'Connor, a psychic healer, who would be speaking about the "other side" and giving messages from departed loved ones to the audience. I decided to do a pre-interview on the phone to assess her. After a few minutes of small talk about her work as a medium, she told me she had a message for me and asked if she could share it.

"Sure, I'm open," I said, curious.

"Your maternal grandmother is here, and she's singing happy birthday. Does that make sense? I glanced at my calendar and realized it was August 10th, Grandma Vargo's birthday.

"Oh my gosh, it would have been her birthday today." I was ready to hear more.

"She says she watches over you and wants you to remember not to wear the crown of thorns. You are here to spread light...wait did you just lose a baby?"

"Yes." The reminder hurt, but this time she said my spirit guides were talking, not Grandma.

"That baby was not meant to incarnate in human form. That soul came to raise the vibration of your womb so you could carry the next child, who will be a very evolved soul."

As someone who'd grown up with a traditional Christian background, this message was over the top for me, but I couldn't deny how it somehow made me feel better. I would rather think there was a spiritual reason for all the pain we were going through, even if it sounded off the wall.

"Okay, when will I have another healthy baby?" I asked hoping more than anything that would happen.

Kerrie answered me without hesitation. "There is a strong male energy around you. You will conceive sometime between December and January of this year. The nine month cycle of the baby will be the birth of a new cycle in your life."

Needless to say, I booked Kerrie for the show. I wouldn't know how accurate the messages were until I found out I was pregnant again on New Year's morning, 2009. I'd had my suspicions, but decided to wait to take the test until New Year's, since Dennis and I both had the day off, and I was hoping for something to celebrate.

I ran downstairs to the living room, where Dennis was sitting. "I'm pregnant."

He turned around and looked up at me with a wide smile. "What? Are you sure?"

I nodded, wearing a big grin. "I bought a test, hoping we could ring in the New Year with good news."

The doctors told us to wait six months after losing the baby before getting pregnant again, and we had just crossed the threshold. Once again, conceiving was the easy part, though I now worried carrying the baby would be the tough part.

After giving me a big hug, Dennis picked up Helena, who was now almost two years old. "You're going to be a big sister!"

I couldn't wait to tell my father. Dennis and I thought he could keep a secret, so I spilled the beans: "Dad, I'm pregnant again!"

"Hot damn! That's great news, Kara. Hot damn!" I could hear the relief in his excitement. I'm sure he worried I may not have been able to have a healthy baby again. I know we did.

"Now listen, Dad, you can't tell anyone yet because it's too early."

"Okay, yes ma'am! I won't say a thing."

I wore big clothes to work, and didn't tell people I was pregnant until I was five months along, just in case. I'm sure people could tell, but after what we had been through, no one asked.

Julian Crescenzo Stephen House was born one week early on September 1, 2009. Dad was now eighty-nine, and was, once again, at the hospital waiting to meet his new grandchild along with our mothers and Soozie. Unlike Helena, everyone said Julian looked like Dad, with long skinny legs, curly blonde hair (Similar to Dad's baby pictures), and a big presence that far exceeded his tiny body. In time, it became clear he had a personality like Dad, too, since everything he did was big and bold. His tantrums were fierce, his cries for food were extra loud as he banged his fists on the high chair tray, and his giant crystal blue eyes seemed to contain the hidden wisdom of an old soul.

Even my mother took notice. "Julian has a lot of Bruce in him."

She was right, but we still kept our promise to honor our mothers' sides with his middle names—Crescenzo for Marilyn's father, and Stephen after my maternal grandfather, who had taken such great care of me when I was a baby.

My father loved holding Julian and clunking his head on Julian's forehead with a "boom, boom." Julian always cracked up, wanting more, even though I worried about his tiny skull.

"This baby is rugged, he can handle it," Dad would say.

The two of them bonded, tethered by their toughness. As Julian grew, his hair came in platinum white, and random women would stop us on the street to touch it, and sometimes kiss his head in between gushes of, "look at the hair on that beautiful baby…"

He fit in perfectly at Bailey's Beach in Newport, where towheads were part of the summer landscape. Every weekend we took the kids to the beach to meet my father for lunch. The days of sitting for long drawn out conversations over dessert on comfortable upholstered cushions were over. Dad had to get used to the idea of sacrificing a white linen table for French fries on the plastic chairs closer to the sand, where children were supposed to sit.

At this stage in his life, family trumped formality, and he loved every second he spent with our children—though sometimes he looked at us in disbelief as Julian screamed in his high chair: "Can't you make him quiet down? What's wrong?" Dad asked, looking worried and concerned, not understanding that Julian was known for loud dramatic wails on an hourly basis.

"He just doesn't want to sit anymore," I would answer, exasperated, hoping my father would get the message to eat a little faster so we could leave. "Den, can you just take him for a sec and I'll sit with Dad?"

"Sure, uh oh, um..." a look of dread coming over his face.

"What's wrong now?" Dad asked, clearly oblivious to the smell coming from our sweet child.

"Oh God, he exploded...it's leaking..." I said, wondering how to get him out of the lunch room without everyone losing their lunch.

Den moved in for the rescue swooping him out of the high chair, "I got him," he said, running to the bathroom with arms outstretched, trying to keep the leak from springing on him.

"Is there anything I should do to help?" Dad asked, looking helpless.

"Not unless you can change a diaper," I laughed. This was not a crisis he could battle, and he clearly didn't want to be in this particular foxhole.

After a weekend of watching us in toddlerdom, Dad sent us one of his trademark letters, dictated to his secretary and typed on his official letterhead, thanking us for a joyful weekend with the children.

"Dennis, you are the best "mother" I have ever seen in a father. I'm amazed at how you take care of Helena and Julian. If it weren't for nannies, I don't know how my three boys would have survived."

Dad admitted he had never changed a diaper in his life and wasn't sure if he had even held a bottle. It just wasn't what men like him did, especially in his generation. I decided there should be a first for everything, and if Dad had never fed a baby, then this was his time to learn. I placed my large chunky towhead son on Dad's lap and handed him a Doctor Brown's bottle filled with baby formula. "Okay, Dad, hold his head up a bit and give him the bottle. Believe me, he'll take it."

Dad was the very picture of nerves as he placed the plastic nipple near Julian's mouth, seeming very unsure of himself. For a man who'd always been in control of every situation and used to issuing commands, Dad's look of vulnerability in the hands of a baby was utterly charming. Julian's tiny strong hands grasped the bottle, and he started to suck the milk down at his usual rapid pace. Julian was happy having his Poppy feed him, smiling back as the milk dribbled out the corners of his mouth onto Dad's fingers.

As Julian grew old enough, he loved to talk to women. "Hey, ladies," he'd yell at the power walkers passing by in the neighborhood.

"Oh, look at how cute he is."

Julian had Dad's magnetism and Dennis's likeability.

As Dad's traits grew more apparent in my son, I felt relief knowing a part of my father would always be with me through Julian, regardless of how much longer he lived. I would never be ready to lose my father, but there was some solace knowing he got to witness a part of himself be born in my son.

Four months after Julian's birth, we all gathered for my father's 90th birthday at the Providence Performing Arts Center. Dad had helped build the center to become the first-rate theater it is today, and they honored him with a party for five hundred people. I produced and narrated a video showcasing the highlights of Dad's career and family life, even joking about my own arrival thirteen years earlier. The soundtrack to the story was a song I knew he loved, that summed up his life. Dad had always told me and my brothers, "When I die I want, 'I Did It My Way' played at my funeral." Dad loved Sinatra, and made a rare confession: "Of everything I have known, if I could be born again, I'd choose to be able to sing."

He couldn't carry a tune in a suitcase, and unfortunately neither can I. But that night we were in perfect harmony — he loved my tribute and publicly thanked me when he got up to the podium to speak.

"I want to thank all of you for coming tonight. It's been nice to hear such wonderful things said about me, and I want to invite you all back here to celebrate my 100th birthday."

I planned on it, since Dad always got what he wanted.

21 CROSSING OVER

As I approached my 19th Father's Day with Dad, now ninety-one, I got the call I'd feared the most. Dennis and I were enjoying a rare date night in Newport. The first time Soozie called, I let it go to voicemail, figuring I'd get back to her when we were done with dinner. Then she called Dennis's cell phone.

"Hi, Soozie..." I said wondering what was so urgent and hoping it wasn't anything bad.

"Kara, honey...." she was clearly crying, "you need to come to Rhode Island Hospital. Your father has been rushed to the emergency room. There is something wrong, and he's in a lot of pain."

"Oh God," I said, feeling sick. "Okay, we're leaving now. We're in Newport, so I'm only thirty minutes away." Years of reporting on death and destruction had trained me to hover above horror so I could gather important information. But this was *my dad*. The blood drained out of me as I looked at Dennis. "We have to go, my dad is in the hospital." I tried to keep calm on the thirty minute ride to the emergency room.

"What's wrong with him?" Dennis asked.

"They don't know, something with his stomach. He's in a lot of a pain." We ditched our car in the parking garage of the hospital and ran the rest of the way to find Dad lying in a hospital bed.

He smiled weakly at the touch of my hand on his shoulder. "Hey, Dad." Looking at Soozie's puffy eyes, I put on an encouraging smile.

"Hi, baby," he winced in obvious pain. "Thank you for coming. I hope it wasn't too much trouble."

"Oh, Dad," I whispered, struggling to hide my tears, "of course not."

The doctor came in and explained that one of my father's kidneys was blocked and he'd need an operation to drain it...immediately. The good news was they had caught it in time before anything toxic happened to his insides.

I let out a sigh of relief, knowing there was a plan to help my father. It was a routine procedure, and the docs seemed confident Dad would be out in a couple of days. It sounded encouraging, but I couldn't help wondering about what surgery would do to a ninety-one-year-old man. But the doctors were confident Dad's risks were minimal because of his amazing health for his age—no heart conditions and the blood pressure of a teenager.

Dad was pretty cocky about his health, and loved to shout from the rooftops how healthy and strong he was: "C'mon I'll put my numbers up against anyone and win," he would gloat after getting a physical.

His good spirits raised my own, and we laughed in the prep room as I snapped pictures of him smiling in his hospital gown to text to my brothers. Dad was in good spirits, and all seemed fine going into the operating room. Unfortunately, the simple procedure wasn't enough. They discovered the other kidney was blocked, too, and wanted to perform another operation to insert another stent in a few days. I stayed on to help Dad recover. He didn't make for the best patient: He hated the IV's and catheter, and would constantly tug at the tubes, which made life tough for the nurses. "I'm in pain! Get these off of me!"

Soozie and I tried everything to calm him down. "C'mon, Dad, just let them lead—they know best how to take good care of you. Remember your motto: Lead, follow, or get out of the way!"

I wished I could have stayed to coach him through the second surgery, but I had already taken a lot of time off, and I knew there would be nothing I could do except sit in the waiting room while the operation was going on. It was more important that I be on hand when he was home recovering, so I went back to hosting my talk show and anchoring the news, always keeping my phone close to me and checking it during commercial breaks.

After the shows, I really wanted to head back to the hospital but, instead, I headed to my interview at The Beyond Center, a place for New Age healing in Vernon, Connecticut.

My photographer, Peter McCue, was always a source of comfort to me at work. His warm smile and open mind made it fun to do stories like this together. But today, as he drove us to the center, he knew I was not myself. "How's your dad?"

"I don't know—I hope ok. He's getting another procedure today, and I'm waiting to hear. I may have to take a call soon.

"Okay. If you need to slip out, I can cover." Peter was always a master at making me feel better. He seemed to understand that I desperately wished the world would stop turning and let me off for a bit so I could be with Dad.

I was set to interview the owner and psychic medium, Rebecca Anne LoCicero, about her weekly events to help people heal with "messages from the beyond." Instead, it seemed my father was trying to send me a message from the hospital.

As we neared the end of the interview, the psychic asked me if I had a sister who passed.

"Yes, my stepsister, Cintra," I said, silently reflecting on her suicide years earlier. She'd been Dad's stepdaughter with Joy, his third wife—and she'd been the closest thing I'd had to a sister. Years later, I still missed her.

"She says in this family, it's just sister—no 'step.' "

I almost laughed, because she had always been adamant about that. "True—that's right."

"She wants to be there for you now." Before I could say anything, she closed her eyes, then opened them. "You're worried about your Dad?"

Chills spread across my arms as I nodded. "He's in surgery now."

A strange look came over her face,

"I'm getting something from him now..." she said.

"Huh?" I said, confused, "But Dad's still with us."

She explained that energy knows no boundaries, and a soul's energy can communicate when it's still alive.

Peter and I sat silent, waiting to hear more.

"He doesn't like all the tubes—he's showing me how he pulls out the tubes. He's a man who likes to be in control, right?"

"Yes," I said eagerly.

"You need to help him feel like he's more in control—he doesn't like everyone forcing him to do these procedures, and he says it has to be on his terms."

"Sounds like Dad."

It was a fascinating interview, and as we walked back to the car, I thought more about what she'd said about Dad. I thought she'd been referring to the IV tubes he'd hated with a passion, until I got back to the car and my phone rang—it was Soozie, and she was crying.

She told me they couldn't do the surgery on my father because he wouldn't let them put the tubes in his back—he kept yanking at the cords and was combative with the nurses and doctors. I started crying, too, not only because I knew Dad needed that surgery, but because I realized he had reached out to me through the psychic five minutes before. She had just described the exact scene that was playing out at the hospital while I was doing the interview.

Peter and I sat dumbfounded, both thinking there was no way the psychic could have known all that.

The only thing I knew for sure was that I needed to get to that hospital immediately and help settle my father and let the doctors do their job. Ever the fighter, he was inadvertently destroying his chances for a good outcome. He was definitely picking the wrong battles.

The doctors had only used local anesthesia because of Dad's age. Next time, they would have to put him out, and I knew I had to be there.

Thankfully, my bosses understood, and I sped off to RI hospital to hopefully talk some sense into Dad. When I arrived, still wearing my high heels and brightly colored skirt and blouse for TV, he seemed happy to see me, cracking a smile as he weakly extended his hand for me to hold.

His frail appearance scared me, and I went on a mission to make him eat. I brought him apple pastries from Au Bon Pain, hoping to prey on his sweet tooth, but he only took a nibble and said, "No more...take me home."

"Can't do that."

I resorted to acting like a drill sergeant, demanding he down at least a can of syrupy Ensure that the nurses said was filled with vitamins. "Dad don't you want to get out of here?"

"Yes!"

"Then drink!"

The doctors wanted to insert a PICC line to feed Dad nutrients and painkillers, but were concerned he would fight them off—and it needed to be inserted at the exact right angle through his arm and into his chest.

"Dad, I'm going to be right here, and we're going to get this done, okay?"

"Okay." He seemed tired of the fight and wanted to just get back to sleep.

I had never seen my father so listless. I held his arm and hand, and talked him through the delicate procedure—and after thirty minutes, the doctors had what they needed: a pathway into Dad's body to deliver fuel during his next operation. Hurrah!

The surgery went well, and I felt sure we would now be able to get Dad to focus on getting better. He just needed to tap into that inner strength that gushed like a geyser whenever it erupted. I was positive Dad could heal himself—he just needed a push. They sent him to a rehab center, and I visited almost daily, trying to get him to listen to the physical therapists and do his exercises.

"Come on, Dad, you always tell me how strong you are, so prove it." My intent was to engage his competitive spark, but all he wanted to do was sleep. His temperature rose, and they sent him back to the hospital, worried that he had an infection.

I was filled with dread…oh no, no, no, not one more thing. I mustered up all the strength I had and prayed for him to heal. I begged the universal force that had always guided me to now help me find the answers we needed for his health—but that proved elusive. Dad's body was shutting down, and my heart broke when I realized it was time to call my brothers and tell them to fly in. Until now, we all thought Dad would beat this—because he always did—but the doctors told us if he went home, he would need constant care, and that he might not ever be a hundred percent again. He'd simply lost too much strength. But I took what they'd said with a grain of salt, because they just didn't know my dad and his ability to fight.

In the meantime, Soozie slept at the hospital on a pull-out bed each night, and my father's ex-wife, Marjorie, stopped by daily with treats and get-well gifts. We joked to the nurses that we were a happily dysfunctional family. Both of my father's wives, and me— the surprise daughter—traded shifts to make sure Dad wasn't alone.

Dad's spirits lifted when my brothers arrived. They sat around his hospital bed and told him stories about the latest happenings in their lives. We enjoyed family meals of to-go sandwiches and lemonade at the foot of Dad's bed, and settled on a care plan for after he left the hospital. All of us chose to believe he would be the exception to the rule and be back to his old self soon. The doctors were pleased with Dad's reports, so I felt safe to go back to work, and my brothers flew back to home.

I'd only been back to work one day when Soozie called me in tears. It was Tuesday morning, July 19th. "Kara, your father has taken a turn for the worse, and the doctors feel you should come back."

"I'm on my way," I said through sobs.

As I drove, I thought about the past few weeks. He'd had two surgeries to unblock his kidneys, and had spent most of that time in excruciating pain. I knew he was exhausted. I thought about Dad's and my journey and how we'd made the most of every moment after we decided we really did love each other. How could I ever live without that?

I made the familiar trek to Dad's room, but this time it felt different. His hug lingered, and I started to cry. *Does he know he's leaving me?* I had worked so hard to find my dad, and I couldn't face going back to a world without him. I buried my face in his hospital gown and let it all go—I melted into him, my heart silently begging him to keep on going, yet knowing he couldn't. I wanted him to live to see my children grow up, to watch my career grow, to campaign for Dennis when he runs for office someday. The ticking Dad-clock I had felt before was getting louder and about to ding, and there was so much more I wanted to say and do. I wasn't finished yet.

I wanted my nightly phone calls, family vacations, and history lessons. I wanted arguments over what's appropriate dress at a Newport dinner, formal invitations to holidays, and most of all, his love—the love that always made me strong and inspired me to do more. I had a beautiful family of my own to take care of, but I didn't know how I would go on without my rock—the boulder that I'd had chiseled open to create a safe place to heal. Together, we had strengthened each other, changed each other's identity, and created a life that was better than either of us could have imagined.

If he died, I feared I might collapse, unable to ever move again. But, somehow, I understood his hug was letting me know that we would do this part together, too. I would help him die on his terms. I would be the one he needed in the foxhole, making sure his exit strategy was carried out.

One of those strategies involved letting his old staff know the end was near. My father considered his time as governor as the best days of his life, and many of his staff were still among his closest friends twenty years later. Predictably, the old crew showed up in droves—so many that I lost count. Among the crowd was Senator Sheldon Whitehouse, who was my father's director of policy when he was governor,; his former press secretary, Barbara Cottam; Chief of staff, David Preston; and, of course, his faithful friend and assistant, Patti Goldstein. I gave her a long hug, remembering all the secret talks we'd had before the rest of the world knew about me.

David Morsilli looked at me with tears in his eyes. After driving me to me meet my father for the first time, and then becoming my boyfriend, he had witnessed our transformational journey firsthand. "I'm so sorry, Kara, I know how much you two love each other."

Dad perked up with each visit, talking more than he had in days, clearly loving talking about the good old times. All the reminiscing made it seem like he was improving, but when the crowds were gone, so was his voice. He had given his last meet and greet—his last rally before moving on. Fifi had come to the hospital, and we both slept on chairs outside his room, too afraid to leave.

The next day, Dad stopped moving or talking. When the doctors asked us what we wanted, Soozie and I agreed we wanted him to come home. He had been begging to go home for three weeks, and we knew he'd want to die in his house. The doctor wasn't as agreeable and warned Dad could die on the way, but we had to at least try. My dad had managed to escape from the Nazis, and we knew he wanted to escape from this hospital. Tracy arrived breathless from the airport, and we all agreed that we were the people he needed in his final foxhole. The old staff banded together and assumed their old roles of advance team, security, and press secretary to handle the rumors swirling that Governor Sundlun was dying.

Soozie and I operated like a stealth military unit, rushing Dad's limp sleeping body into the ambulance on a scorching hot July day. A team of state troopers escorted us to Dad's home in Jamestown, making sure we wouldn't get stuck in beach traffic.

I called Dennis, who was on the way to the hospital with his mother, Marilyn, and told them to turn around, "I need you to meet us at my dad's house; we're taking him home."

"Okay, what do you need me to do?"

"Clear out his office, the hospice nurses need a place to set up a bed."

My adrenaline was pumping as Soozie and I held on to either side of dad's stretcher. I leaned down and whispered in his ear. "You're going to be okay, Dad. You're going home, just like you wanted."

Dad and Soozie's seaside house sat on top of a hill, overlooking Naragansett Bay, and the only way in was up a flight of stairs. It took the strength of several men to carefully move the stretcher up the steep stairs and into his study, where they placed his unconscious body onto the bed the hospice nurses had provided. I willed myself not to collapse in a pool of tears. It seemed like just yesterday when we'd shared our first hello.

I didn't know what to do next. I'd never seen anyone die before, and I could only think of reading *Tuesday's with Morrie*, by Mitch Albom, where he talked about how the dying needed you talk to them, love them, and witness the end of their life. I wanted to do all that for Dad. We called up one of his dearest friends, Nuala Pell, the widow of the late Senator Claiborne Pell to let her know the end was near, and she rushed over to say a final goodbye. Mrs. Pell was the embodiment of graciousness, and it was good to see her kind face as we let her have a moment alone with Dad. After she left, it seemed Dad was slipping further away.

"What do we do now?" I asked the hospice nurse.

"Just wait. The end will probably be here soon, his breathing is getting slow. Is he waiting for anyone?"

"What do you mean?"

"Sometimes they hang on waiting to say goodbye."

"My two other brothers, Peter and Stuart, weren't able to catch flights in time, but Tracy and his daughter, Fifi, are here."

"Maybe you should call the others—the hearing is the last thing to go."

I went back into the study where we were all holding vigil around Dad.

Tracy and I took the nurses advice and used his cell phone to call Stuart, pressing the phone against Dad's ear so he could say his final goodbyes. Though Dad's eyes were closed, I felt sure he heard his son's loving words. We did the same with Peter. And finally Soozie's son, Max, called in to give his tearful farewell. When it was over, all we could do was wait.

"Dad, we're all here, and we love you," I said, stroking his beautiful hair.

Soozie whispered, "Just relax, sweetheart, your mom and dad are waiting for you. I know your dad and you didn't always get along but he's much nicer over there, plus your crew from the war is waiting." Her daughter, Heather, stroked her back trying to comfort Soozie.

As the intervals between his breaths grew longer, we waited, wondering each time if it was his last one. "Dad, you made us a family, and we promise to always take care of each other and Soozie. It's okay for you to go." My tears dripped on his cheek.

On July 21, 2011, Dad took his final breath. At the same time, the outside door blew open and a picture flew off the wall. We instantly knew he had just left the Earth with his trademark gusto.

We were all stunned silent. The door was one they never used, and there was no wind on this hot-humid afternoon.

"I guess they came and got him," Tracy said, gazing at the blown-open door.

Soozie's son-in-law, Ray, shook his head in dismay. "If I hadn't seen this myself, I wouldn't have believed it."

Tears streamed down Soozie's face while she caressed Dad's cheek. "He must have found the light."

Sure, I believed in an afterlife, but until this moment I had never witnessed such a powerful example of it. I hugged my Dad's still-warm body and silently thanked him for the signs.

As if the door blowing open wasn't enough, Dad was sending us signs with numbers — 91, in particular. He was 91 years old, it was 91 degrees out, and when we looked for a blanket to cover him, we found one someone had sent him as a thank you gift with an American bald eagle and the number 91 in the corner, signifying the year he took office. I felt comforted — as if Dad was watching over us.

"I can't believe the 91's. It just can't be a coincidence," Tracy said, looking baffled.

But we all agreed, and knew it would always be a special number for all of us.

My reporter brain helped me put my grieving on pause, as I realized I needed to help Dad get the sendoff he deserved.

"We need to work up a family statement for the press," I said to Dennis.

"You write it," he said, putting his hand on my shoulder, "and I'll notify the TV stations and the newspaper."

As I sat down to write, it came to me easily,

"Former Governor Bruce Sundlun died peacefully tonight at his home in Jamestown. He was surrounded by his loving family. As a husband, father, and grandfather he was our North Star. We are deeply grateful for his love and lessons throughout our lives."

Dad was my North Star, and I feared the sky would never look as bright without him here. But I wanted to be strong for him. I wanted to make sure we made him proud. I'd like to think we did.

A few moments after Dennis released the statement, the local evening news announced the breaking story that former Governor Bruce Sundlun had died. Since TV stations prepare for moments like these years in advance, the anchors were able to toss in an in depth story on Dad's life. We all watched the newscast and joked that Dad died at the perfect time to be the lead on the evening news.

As news spread, close friends and dignitaries started to call to express their condolences. The then-Congressman Patrick Kennedy considered my father to be one of his mentors and made sure to race to the house before my father's body was taken away.

Exhausted from such an emotionally draining day, I drove to my home in Newport, eager to hug my children and lean on Dennis, who had gone home to be with them, and gather strength for the funeral. Pulling into my driveway, I saw a bright red cardinal sitting on the walkway. When I woke up the next morning, the red bird was the first thing I saw again. I told Soozie when she called to firm up plans for the funeral, and she told me how she kept noticing red cardinals on her path as well. Soozie and I took the cardinal to be a clear sign from Dad, but didn't quite understand the meaning. I now know after doing some research the cardinal symbolizes the highest most important thing in our lives, and Dad was certainly that for me. I still see the cardinal all the time, and know it's Dad fluttering by to say "hey, baby."

Dad's former staff banded together to handle the news reports and the logistics of the kind of funeral we knew Dad would have wanted. The flags flew at half-staff, and his body would lie in state at the Capitol, followed by a public funeral service for the hundreds who would come to mourn him, complete with a military fly over organized by his former legal counsel, Michael Bucci.

Stuart and Peter were on the way, and we would all meet at the funeral home in the morning with Soozie to discuss more details with Rabbi Leslie Gutterman, at Temple Beth El in Providence. Rabbi Gutterman had been a close friend of my father's and was fond of kidding my dad: "Bruce, don't be ashamed you're Jewish, it's bad enough *we're* ashamed you're Jewish!"

Though my father wasn't very religious, he was committed to honoring his heritage, especially since he'd escaped from the Nazis. He had been president of the temple, following in the footsteps of my grandfather, Walter, who'd held the post before him. Rabbi Gutterman insisted on making sure proper Jewish traditions were observed at my father's funeral. He didn't want a media circus, and nixed the idea of playing Frank Sinatra's "I Did It My Way."

"It's fine for the party afterward, but we can't do that during the funeral," he told me firmly.

"But, Rabbi, we have to, it's the only thing my father specifically asked for, and I think we have to honor his wishes."

With a little more coaxing, Rabbi Gutterman agreed to have the organ play the instrumental version of the song, and he would tell the mourners it was my father's wish.

He remained insistent that there be no TV cameras, and I didn't push. Though later, Barbara Cottam, Dad's former press secretary, called to tell us Rabbi Gutterman gave in to having one camera in the temple, since all three television stations planned to broadcast the funeral live. My brothers, Soozie, and I couldn't help but laugh at the thought that Dad must still be pulling strings from the other side.

My brothers and I all agreed to give a brief eulogy, so we could each give our unique reflections of our larger-than-life father. Soozie was understandably too upset to speak, but her children, Max and Heather, wanted to say a few words in her place.

My brothers did a fabulous job of tugging at heart strings and even making people laugh. Tracy opened his eulogy with, "I am Dad's oldest child—or at least we think so..." inviting a laugh out of the crowd.

Stuart recalled a story of when he tried to give Dad a massage. "Stop that, I like the tension."

Peter spoke of Dad's unbelievable accomplishments. "I don't know anyone who has done the body of work Dad has."

Each gave beautiful speeches, without shedding a tear—I knew I couldn't do that. I walked up to the podium, trembling at the thought of bearing my soul on live TV in front of dignitaries, my closest friends, family, and co-workers.

I joked about Dad calling me his new baby out on the campaign trail when we first met, and about following in his footsteps as a broadcaster. But my voice wavered as I neared the end of my notes, and teardrops dampened the ink as they rolled off my nose. "Dad, you were so big in life, that I know, even in death, you won't stop leading us, which is good because I'm lost without you."

I let the pent up tears flow quietly as I took my seat next to Dennis and squeezed Helena's hand to assure her mommy was okay. Then, I listened to Heather and Max talk together about what a force he was in their lives, too. "He truly changed my mother's life...he was loving, passionate, and there was never a dull moment..."

Max said, "You did your best because that's what he expected of you, and he made you better because of it..."

Next came an incredible speech by Senator Sheldon Whitehouse: "He was irrepressible, impatient, imperial, unstoppable, combative, frustrating, willful, constantly threw caution to the wind, impossible to keep up with, he drove us nuts, and we loved him. We loved him because he was bold and brave..."

Sheldon captured my father's essence, and the crowd applauded, knowing Dad would have loved the celebration of his life.

As we walked out past the rows of National Guardsmen standing at attention and saluted my father's flag draped casket, we were struck by a license plate in front of us with just the number 91 on it. We all agreed Dad was letting us know we had made him proud. Dad must have been beaming in heaven. He was the lead story on every newscast, and the next morning the nation's biggest newspapers wrote lengthy obituaries, listing his numerous accomplishments. *The New York Times* headline read, "Rhode Island Governor with Flair, Dies at 91."

The article used a picture of the two of us laughing at my wedding, and went on to say, "Mr. Sundlun cut a larger than life figure that seemed inversely proportional to the size of his state."

Sean Daly, one of my father's all-time favorite local news reporters, gave a live report, saying. "The funeral was as big, and as bold, and as honest as the man himself."

He ended his piece with Helena blowing a kiss as the hearse drove away, an image I will always treasure.

A few days later, with the official mourning over, it was now time for me to go back on TV—the first step in "my life must go on" phase.

My co-host, Scot, hugged me, "You ready?"

I nodded. "I'll have to be."

We usually start the show with some fun stories about our weekend, but we ended up taking up most of our first block talking about the funeral. "It was hands down the best funeral I have ever been to, and I left loving your dad," Scot said as we showed pictures and clips from the service.

After the commercial break, we moved on to other stories, then suddenly the lights in the studio went out leaving us completely in the dark.

In five years of doing the show, I can't remember ever having to stop for something like this.

A crew member yelled out, "There's something wrong with light number 91."

Scot and I sat stunned. Really? Number 91?

"Kara's dad just wants us to keep talking about him," Scot joked.

Dad let me know he was with me on my first day back.

22 Full Circle in His Footsteps

Jabbeke, Belgium: September 19, 2013

Just when I thought I had cried enough and learned all I needed to about my dad, the Universe sent me the lesson of compassion. How can we understand another's plight until we walk in their shoes?

The World War II Foundation had decided to produce a documentary film on my father's heroic escape from Nazi territory. The founder, Tim Gray, wanted me to travel to Belgium to retrace Dad's steps so he could tell the story through my perspective. Dad was showing me the final puzzle piece to who he was.

Traveling with a photographer and producer, we arrived at the Brussels train station after a long journey from Boston through Paris. The documentary was about my father, but I had no idea how this experience of escaping the Nazis would open my eyes to truly understanding him. I scanned the pick-up area near outside the train station for Luc Packo. He was the Belgian who had spent his life recording the history of my father's crew aboard the *Damn Yankee*, the B-17 Flying Fortress that crashed into Luc's small village of Jabbeke, near Brugge, on December 1, 1943. I had no idea that I was about to meet a man who seemed to love my father as much as I did.

"Kara, Kara," he called from somewhere near the taxi stand where I was waiting.

My jet-lagged eyes searched the crowd of well-dressed Europeans bustling around the station and found Luc, a tall, strong stocky man with blonde hair and crystal blue eyes walking toward me with his son Jens, equally tall and blonde.

I hugged each of them. "Thank you so much for helping us with the film. We are so grateful you will help us tell my father's story."

His voice was heavy with emotion. "It is my honor. I have deep respect for your father, so this is an honor for me and my family."

I introduced Luc to the crew, Tim Gray, the chairman of the World War II Foundation and the producer of the film, and Jim Karpeichik, the photographer. We then got into Luc's small SUV and began the journey to retrace my father's steps.

The weather was raw, with a wet chill in the air and grey skies. We were all relieved to be in the hands of our guide, Luc, as we relaxed in the backseat.

Luc looked at me through the rearview mirror. "You know you look like your father."

I smiled. "Yes, I am told that a lot. Thanks."

My being here made all the sense in the world. This was my father's story. But I couldn't understand why Luc was so excited to give up four days of his life to be our tour guide. "Luc, how did you become so interested in the story of the *Damn Yankee*?" I asked.

"Since I was a boy of twelve, I would go to the field in my village and search for pieces of your father's plane. It has become my passion to tell the story of the Americans like your father who liberated our people. We have him to thank for our freedom."

Though Luc was born in 1964, a generation after World War II, his life pivoted around the history of that time. For all these years, he had gone to the field where my father's plane crashed and collected remains of the plane: screws, nuts, bolts, pieces of Plexiglas. Sometimes the years of searching would bring a great find, like a broken off piece of the pilot's radio that my father might have worn. Though Luc made a living working in a metal factory, his life revolved around researching how the Americans liberated

Belgium from the poverty and slave labor camps imposed by the Germans. Specifically, he told me of his fascination with my father's plane, *Damn Yankee*, and its crew.

This man, who had no personal connection to my father, had devoted his life, money, and vacation time to honoring Dad and his crew. As a young American who had never witnessed war on my land, the deep gratitude he had for Americans was deeply moving.

Entering Jabbeke, the roads turned into a cobblestone ribbon that wound its way to picturesque Belgian homes with their tile roofs, sculpted boxwood hedges, and manicured yards. I looked out at the beautiful countryside, trying to imagine my father searching for help. Cows grazed lazily in the green pastures, a perfect reflection of the relaxed way the Europeans lived. There was such natural beauty here, and I was instantly taken by the unhurried pace and peace here. It was a stark contrast to my American urge to rush and check my cell phone.

Luc pulled up in front of the historic Haeneveld Hotel. "I hope you like where I have chosen for you. It is my favorite hotel in my village."

"I love it," I said, instantly charmed. "It's really beautiful. Thank you so much."

Tim and Jim were raring to go, so after a quick break to check in and dump our luggage, we set out to survey the town for places where we needed to shoot.

One of our first stops was the first Catholic church my father went to in Brugge the night he escaped. My father had always told me the Catholic church saved his life because, after the crash, he escaped the Nazis by stealing bicycles and going from church to church across Europe. "When I was in high school, my track coach told me some day I'd be in trouble and that I should find a priest. If he couldn't help me, then he'd know someone who could."

While Tim and Jim surveyed the area, I went inside the chapel to light a candle for my father. In that moment, I could feel him with me. *What do I need to learn here?* I wondered? My father's war stories had always seemed so unreal, like a fantasy about another world so different from mine, but now standing in the very same church my father had seventy years earlier, his journey was coming to life for me. I tried to see it through his eyes and imagined my father's relief at the priest's offer to help him by connecting him to the Resistance. My father had told me that every church was the same; the priest would bring in a low level criminal, like a thief or a prostitute, to help him because they knew how to avoid the Germans. Since he had no papers, he couldn't travel by car. Since he stood out as an American, he couldn't be seen in public, so he had to get creative.

I still remember the story: "I learned pretty quickly the women bought bread at the same time every day. While they went into the bakery, I would steal a tall woman's bicycle and ride away as fast as I could to the next town."

He traveled this way all the way through Belgium and France, and finally made it safely to neutral Switzerland.

Instead of going home and enjoying his freedom, he showed his true warrior DNA by joining the Resistance to continue fighting the Germans. As fate would have it, he ended up in the mountains with Allen Dulles, who'd recruited him, and became a spy for the Office of Strategic Services, which was the precursor to the CIA.

Even though I'd known all this before, it finally struck me, standing in this church where he'd stood so many years ago, that Dad's early resolve to fight matched the force he'd used on me at first by trying to battle my existence, or his responsibility to me. His nature was to fight, and he'd spent a lifetime building up coats of armor around his heart. It served him well to survive the war, but those barriers prevented him from accepting love in his life. The casualties of that pattern had been his five marriages, and my growing up fatherless.

I suddenly felt his presence: *"Kara, you had to teach me how to open my heart."*

While the crew continued to get shots for the film, my own script was being written. I was trying to fill in my own blanks and understand my father—what made him the man he was before I knew him.

The next morning, we headed out early to the place I was most looking forward to—the field where my father's plane crashed. Jim got the camera ready as I put on my microphone and headed out into the field with Luc.

"Your father's plane started coming in over there," he said pointing to an adjacent cornfield. "Five men had already died, he told the other four to bail out."

I imagined my father in a crashing plane all alone, and cringed.

"Unfortunately," Luc continued, "the men landed right where German soldiers were doing military exercises, and they were all captured. Your father bailed out here, and by the time his parachute opened, he was nearly on the ground, and he was hurt and bleeding."

"What happened next?" I asked, clinging to his every word.

"A farmer and a man from the Resistance were in the field and helped your father bury his parachute. They knew the Germans would be looking for him."

"What would have happened to them if they got caught?'

"They would have been executed for helping an American."

It was just so hard to take in, how strangers risked their own lives so my father could live.

"Your father had no time, the Germans were coming, and he needed to hide."

I remembered what happened next, because Dad had told me this part of the story himself: "I remembered Edgar Allen Poe's *The Purloined Letter* and hiding things in plain sight, so I dug myself in between two furrows in the field and blended in with the landscape."

According to Luc, that flash of inspiration likely saved his life.

"He lay there until dark, wounded on his shoulder from the flak. The Germans passed right by him, but they didn't see him."

My dam of professionalism evaporated in front of the camera, and tears erupted down my cheeks, making it hard for me to speak. "He must have been so scared," I sobbed. "It makes me so sad to think he was bleeding all alone in a ditch, not knowing what happened to his crew."

Sadness coursed through me. Standing in the very field where he'd landed and hid, I understood why he rarely talked about his experiences. Facing death does that to a person.

Luc wrapped his big arms around me. I knew the cameras were still rolling, but I felt like Dad was standing next to me, reliving it all. It was a lot to absorb.

I took a minute to regroup, then asked him to tell me what happened after my father came out of hiding.

"He saw two young boys carrying a wagon with leaves and realized he'd frightened them because he was big and bloodied. He won them over by giving one of the boys some gum and the other, his pocket knife. 'English, English,' your father said. The boys pointed to a nearby barn and your father went running. He met a tool salesman man at the gate who motioned for him to go inside, knowing the people who lived there would help him. He banged on the door, and the man of the house let him in, much to the chagrin of his pregnant wife, who was screaming at him for putting her family in danger, and for messing up her clean floors." Luc stopped and let out a small chuckle. "Anyway, despite her anger, she went to work on your father's wounds."

"I remember this part," I told Luc. "Dad told me about it, saying she scrubbed his wounds with alcohol and a toothbrush. He swore he could still feel the pain."

"Tomorrow I take you there," Luc said. "You can meet the man who was at the gate."

"I can't wait to thank him for saving his life," I said. How many people got the chance to personally thank someone for being brave enough to get involved? This was an honor—a debt I could never repay.

Luc guided me to the field to look for pieces of the wreckage from my father's plane. "I find something every time I come."

It seemed unrealistic that we would discover something right then with cameras rolling—that would be too perfect. "Come on, Dad, help me find a piece of your plane today to bring home," I said laughing, but secretly praying for his help.

At that very moment, Luc stooped down to grab something from the dirt. "Plexiglas. This is from your father's plane. The windows and windshield of the B-17 were made of Plexiglas." He grabbed a piece of regular glass to show me the difference. "You see this is shiny and not from the plane. This is Plexiglas, so it must come from the *Damn Yankee*."

I fingered the tiny fragment in my hand, moving it about to catch the light. I held it out, so Jim could get a shot of it. "Thanks Dad," I whispered. "I knew you'd want me to have that."

It was becoming clear to me that my trip was multi-faceted. We were sent to do a story on my father's crash and harrowing journey to safety, but the human side to his fight came crashing in on me. Dad's stories had always taken on a romanticized tone of glory when briefly told around the dinner table. But here, I could feel his fear, his determination, wondering if he'd make it home alive.

Here, I suddenly understood why I'd had to wage a battle to make him open up to me. Fighting from a place of fear was natural for him. Coming from a lighter place of love wasn't within his comfort zone. Just like he would flinch if you came up behind him, or refused to sit in a restaurant with his back to the door, his fears had manifested into a massive defense system, and I was seeing where at least part of that fear was born. My tears for his twenty-three-year-old self birthed a new path of compassion for him in my own heart. We had already grown to love each other, and I had forgiven him long before, but now I *understood* him in a way I had not been able to before.

As humans, we are shaped by our experiences, and our reactions are formed by what we face. My father had learned at an early age to circumvent the heart and react from his place of fight or flight. This forcefulness had helped him in war and in business, but it had failed him in matters of the heart, where vulnerability is required.

While I was trying to internalize my newfound view of my father, my oldest brother Tracy arrived. He had decided last minute to join us in Belgium, knowing the chance to retrace our father's steps was a once in a lifetime experience.

Luc couldn't take his eyes off Tracy. "Oh my, you look so much like your father."

"Yes, except I'm not as smart and have less hair," Tracy said, laughing.

The truth was, he was brilliant, just like Dad, but was much warmer and less intimidating. I wondered how Tracy felt, standing in the very place that made his father a hero and had shaped him into the tough demanding father Tracy had spent a lifetime trying please.

Before I had the chance to ask, Luc showed Tracy the monument with the names of everyone who'd died in the crash, and I could see the emotion well up in his eyes. The monument's inscription was written in Dutch. "Can you read it for me, please?"

Luc translated: "It says, 'Here on December 1st 1943, an American B-17 Bomber 'Flying Fortress' crashed. Five crew members were killed. Five young men died for our freedom.' "

Tracy ran his fingers over the inscription and shook his head. "It's just unbelievable."

I was grateful Tracy and I could experience this together. It was like Dad was showing us something he had never been able to tell us when he was alive. He'd resisted so much in his life. Me, for one, his toughness toward my brothers, and his discomfort with matters of the heart—they were effects of what had happened here. He had returned home a hero, but he'd carry the bullet in his heart, where no one could see. It was not okay for his generation to express fear or share their grief.

I was starting to understand why my father liked to say he only cared about "Who, what, where, when, how—the *why* doesn't matter." For Dad, the *why* was subjective, based on people's opinion and not the facts. Maybe *why* was too painful or frightening.

To me, standing on this field with Tracy, the *why* was everything and the exact answer to so many of my questions. Two years after his death, I had discovered the missing puzzle piece that unlocked the essence of my father's heart, the part of him he had kept locked away so tightly in life.

I cried for him and let him grieve across the veil. My heart felt free. *It's okay, Dad, I understand now, and I love you.* I knew he was with us every step of this journey, and I felt it was healing him as much as it was us.

The next stop was Luc's house. His lovely wife, Karine, a tall blonde woman with a big smile, opened the door and welcomed us into their charming home. I could feel the love in this place— from the carefully manicured yard with its roses and hedges, to the shiny clean tile floors. They had raised five children here after falling in love in high school. Luc and Karine kept apologizing that it wasn't grander. "What your father must have thought when he came here to our common home with our many children and dog," Karine said, still mortified after all those years. She had nothing to apologize for. I saw theirs as a perfect life.

Over lunch of sandwiches, tomato soup, and their local specialty, Hunter's bread, Luc explained he had always wanted to find my father, and couldn't believe it when he saw him on CNN when he became governor. We laughed at the fact that both of us had tracked him down the same way.

"I used to set my alarm to get up in the middle of the night, so I could call him at eight a.m. It took me two years to get hold of him!"

"Don't feel bad, Luc. It took me even longer." Luckily, my father eventually came through for both of us. For Luc, it was when Dad came to Belgium for his book signing in the 90s.

After lunch, Luc brought Tracy, the crew, and me outside to the backyard, where he had set up crates full of fragments from Dad's plane. There were thousands of pieces of bullets, metal fragments, and Plexiglas. The sheer volume was overwhelming. This was Luc's life's work laid out for the cameras to capture, and for us to touch. Some were tiny specs, others big chunks of twisted metal.

I picked up one of the metal fragments and traced it with my fingers. "What's this?"

"It's part of the outside of the plane—see how one side is dark green and the other is lighter? That's how the B-17 was painted."

Luc was like a walking encyclopedia on the plane, deciphering where each tiny piece fit in.

He brought out a wooden box and opened it for me to see. "These are parts of your father's parachute, and these are the clips and what's left of the silk."

"How do you know it's his?" I asked feeling another wave of emotion course through my veins.

"The woman who cleaned his wounds saved it and made clothes. She gave me what was left."

I smiled remembering how Dad loved to tell the story of how he learned the woman used his silk parachute to make a wedding dress for her daughter, something he says he heard on his first trip to meet Luc.

I wished I could take a few more pieces of the plane, but I didn't want to ask, since it was clear every spec of metal meant something to Luc.

Just as we were about to wrap up shooting, Luc brought out a gift for me. Opening the bubble wrap sleeve, I pulled out a shadowbox filled with pieces of my dad's plane. Luc had painstakingly glued down red velvet and attached a bullet, Plexiglas, and two other pieces of metal. He carefully wrote a message on archival paper on the back, recording that these pieces, "came from the B-17 *Damn Yankee* that was shot down December 1, 1943."

Tears stung my eyes as they spilled over and rolled down my cheeks. How could I ever thank him for this beautiful memorial to my father? I had hoped to take home some of Dad's treasures, and Luc had seen to it that I'd have more than just pieces—I'd have a wonderful piece of art for my wall at home.

Even my studio-grade cosmetics couldn't compete with my waterworks.

Tracy had been watching the filming with Luc's family and started to walk toward me, holding out a handkerchief he had taken from his pocket. I took it while laughing and crying all at once. "Seriously," I said in mid-choke, "you are really like Dad. You're the only other person I know to always carry a cotton hankie!"

Tracy laughed and hugged me while I used his Dad-inspired hankie to wipe away the drippy mascara. It was just one more reminder that Dad was with us.

Luc brought us into his kitchen, where he showed us four giant binders filled with more stuff on Dad. Luc had saved every article, e-mail, even Christmas cards, and put them in protective plastic sleeves in the binders. As I skimmed through the pages, I saw Luc even had the articles about me uniting with Dad at the news conference, and my official station bio he had printed off the website. Tracy and I were amazed at how this man—a continent away with no direct connection to our father—had done more to preserve his legacy than we had. My collections of Dad's life were still crammed in a file marked "Dad" in my desk drawer.

"I am *so* going to Staples when I get home and put Dad's stuff in a proper binder," I said, laughing to Tracy.

We hit another emotional landmine when we stumbled across a letter my father had written in 1945 to the sister of one of the women who helped him escape from Jabbeke. My father remembered the sister lived in the U.S., so when he made it home, he found her and wrote her a letter saying how grateful he was to her family for helping him survive. Tracy's voice broke while reading the letter out loud. There wasn't a dry eye in the place, and

I was so happy to be sharing this once-in-a-lifetime experience with him.

I marveled at his neat, legible cursive. How different it was from his trademark illegible handwriting that I'd come to know. I was realizing again there was a man who had existed before he became our father; a man who might have been quite different from the man we knew as war hero, prosecutor, tycoon, governor, and yes, Dad. That man had been shaped by the fears he'd had to face throughout his life, and with each dragon he slew, he became tougher, more powerful — and more removed from his heart.

His sheer determination and will to live and succeed shaped him into a legendary fighter. But he'd spent his life fighting from a place of fear, growing superhero defenses to resist any attacks. I realized this is what he was trying to tell me on this trip. It wasn't *me* he'd resisted back then, but the overwhelming emotions that came with a daughter showing up in his life.

He truly was more afraid of me than a plane losing its engine. He knew how to fight, but loving terrified him. Fortunately, he had passed on his gift of determination to me, and I used that same strength of will to attack him with love. He'd met his match, and I cracked him open with the same force he'd used to resist me. It was all becoming clear to me now that it had to be that way for reasons only our souls understood. Our healing proved the ancient wisdom that love always beats fear. But just because it's meant to be, doesn't mean it's meant to be easy. Twenty years after finding Dad, I found the lost part of him by putting myself in his shoes and literally walking a day in his life. I finally had compassion for the reasons he had shut me out.

Forgiveness is a tunnel to love. Together, across the realms, we have healed each other through an incredible journey. Mission accomplished, I found Dad.

Acknowledgments

I am so grateful to the many people who helped me live out my story and share this book with the world. Above all, I want to thank my mother for always teaching me to follow my heart and that good will come. Her undying love and support, even in the most difficult of times, helped make me who I am today, and her support of this story is why I can tell it.

To my husband, Dennis, for being my best friend and sounding board throughout this process— thank you for always being willing to help me find the time for this journey. To my children, Helena and Julian, I love you more than the whole universe; you both are the joy that keeps me going even after long nights of writing.

To my brothers, Tracy, Stuart, and Peter, I am forever grateful for your always-open hearts, humor, hysterical memories and support of me telling the story of how I found Dad. To Soozie Sundlun, for her love for my father and support of all things spiritual, and the beautiful headshot she took for the book. To Marjorie Sundlun, for opening her heart and home so I could know my father. To Cousin Fenton, I miss you, and thank you for years of comic relief. Of course, to my father who became Dad by showing the world how to right a wrong, and always encouraged me to, "Tell 'em the facts. Don't sugar coat it!"

To my best friends, you are my sisters. To my cousin, Danielle, for car ride calls.

I want to thank the incredible team at Behler Publications for believing in this project and bringing this book to the world especially, Lynn Price, my awe-inspiring editor who honored me by publishing my first book, and challenged me to dig deeper and come from my heart all while making me laugh. Thank you for helping me tell my story in a way I hope will inspire others. To my literary agent, Steven Harris, and Gabriel Harris at CSG literary partners, for your guidance and belief in the importance of my story.

To Mika Brzezinski, for telling me I had to write a book and making me believe I could and should. Without you, this would all still be only a thought. To best-selling author Gabrielle Bernstein for showing me the path. To my long time television agent, Steve Dickstein, who watched my father and I grow over the years and generously offered his wisdom and sage advice on this project.

To my WFSB Channel Three and Meredith family, especially Dana Neves, Patience Hettrick, Klarn DePalma, and Paul Karpowicz for your encouragement always. To my *Better Connecticut* co-host, Scot Haney, for showing me how to bare it all and laugh about it, and our executive producer, Jamie Mascia, for reading the rough drafts and liking it enough to keep reading more. To Denise D'Ascenzo for sharing your wisdom during our green tea and chocolate talks, 444, the angels are always with us.

To Susan Campbell for her valuable class on memoir at the Mark Twain House, and author Diane Smith for sending me there. To Megan Poulin, my writing partner, for making Wednesdays writing night. To Doreen Fishman for helping me still my mind to uncover the real story I needed to tell. To Mariana Cayres, for keeping the little ones happy so I could write.

To Henry Baskin, I am forever indebted to you for helping me reunite with my father and providing me with valuable details needed to tell my story twenty years later. To Patti Goldstein, for your keen reflections. To G. Wayne Miller at the *Providence Journal* for your many great articles on my father and help with some of the photos in this book.

About the Author

Kara Sundlun is an Emmy Award winning television journalist. She anchors the news for WFSB-TV, the CBS affiliate in Connecticut and hosts the popular daytime talk show *Better Connecticut*. Her series Kara's Cures is a mainstream guide to health and spirituality, she is also a contributor for the Huffington Post.

Kara was named "Best Reporter" by Hartford Magazine, "Top 40 under 40" Hartford Business Journal and Connecticut Magazine, and is a board member for Dress for Success Hartford.
She is married to fellow news anchor Dennis House and mom to cherished children Helena and Julian.

To find out more about Kara and the amazing journey with her father, be sure to visit her webpage:
www. karasundlun.com